THE GOD HYPOTHESIS

A SCIENTIST LOOKS AT RELIGION

F. HENRY FIRSCHING

First Edition, September 1997

Copyright © 1997 by F. Henry Firsching

All Rights Reserved.

Library of Congress Catalog Card Number:
97-90119

International Standard Book Number:
0-9657210-1-9

Think About It Press
5205 Springfield Drive
Edwardsville, IL 62025
(618) 656-4054

TABLE OF CONTENTS

Introduction 1

Chapter 1
An Overall view of Religious Ideas 2
The Grand Delusion 3
The Devil You Say 8
The Beginning of the God Hypothesis 15
Everlasting Life 17
Faith 21
Rules About God 23
Prayer 26
God Fearing 29
Passage to Heaven and Hell 30
God and Punishment 32
Religious Beliefs in General 34

Chapter 2
Implications About the God Hypothesis 37
Variations of the God Hypothesis 38
World Religions 42
The Churches of Today 46
God is Mentioned Everywhere 50
The Habit of Irrational Thought 53
The Destruction of Churches 57
The Holocaust 59
Human Disasters 62
Overall Summary of the Religious Situation .. 65

Chapter 3
Science and Religion 68
The Origin of Life 69
Showing Something Exists 73

The Creation-Evolution Controversy 77
A Wrong Hypothesis 93
Knowable Universe 96
Scientific Analysis of the God Hypothesis 100
Guiding Principles of Science 107
Intelligent Life Elsewhere 112
Chapter 4
Possible Effects of Writing This Book 116
Scientific Personnel 117
Scientist's Thinking 120
The Scientific Community 122
The Religious Community's Response 124
Clergy's Plight 131
Killjoy 131
Conclusion 133

INTRODUCTION

This book is an examination of the concept of god - the god hypothesis. Even though an overwhelming majority of people in the United States believe in god, the reality of this concept has never been demonstrated. People like to believe in god. There can be no doubt that the god hypothesis satisfies a strong human need. But that is not the issue.

The issue in this book is whether the concept is real. Does god really exist? I cannot guarantee any 100% definitive answer, I cannot do that about almost anything. But in the course of this book I will examine many aspects of religion that do not measure up, when compared to reality.

I will not bog down in theology. I am no expert in that area. I will concentrate on facts - scientific facts. As near as anyone can determine, anything that is real can be measured, observed, or its effects observed. If no measurements or observations about a specific item can be obtained, then the item may very well be unreal - imaginary.

I am trying to use common sense in wrestling with a gigantic issue. I try to use everyday examples and logical conclusions about such examples. Hopefully, everything in this book is at a level where scientific expertise is not needed, just common sense.

If this book brings mankind closer to a more realist outlook about life on this earth, then my objectives for writing the book will have been met.

Chapter 1

AN OVERALL VIEW OF RELIGIOUS IDEAS

THE GRAND DELUSION

The best way to start is to define god. The idea of god is vague in many people's minds and different religions often depict god in different ways.

The dictionary definition of god is a supreme being, the creator and master of the universe. This is the concept used in this book. God is the all-powerful being who is master of the entire universe. He has created everything and controls everything.

A god is something that almost everyone wants. It is such a cozy idea. God, the big security blanket, is up there somewhere in the sky, watching over everything. He controls everything, he keeps track of everything, he listens to our prayers and responds to them. He takes care of us and protects us, and most of all, he loves us. The entire scenario reads somewhat like a fairy tale. The fundamental thoughts are exactly the way we want things to be. It sounds almost too good to be true.

One of the first things I will do is go through the basic premises of many religions. These are some of the fundamental ideas of religions in general. I am not an expert on all the religions of the world. Nevertheless, I think I have a fairly good idea of how various religions do operate.

The fundamental idea in almost all religions is the god figure - the god hypothesis. This seems to be a basic premise. Sometimes more than one deity is used, but most often one god is proposed. In this book I will work with the idea of one god.

God is considered to be the creator and master of the universe. He is all-powerful, all-knowing, kind, and righteous. He sees to it that human beings are taken care of and that things go smoothly. It is exactly the way we would like to have events take place. It is so nice to have one great being in control of everything. To know that he is there watching and caring is most comforting. God provides security. God is an ever present watchdog.

Some religions expand the god hypothesis to include angels - god's helpers. Angels do much of the busy work. Even though god is all-powerful, the helping hands of these angels seems to be needed.

Then there is the magical place called heaven - where god resides. Even though god is everywhere around the world all the time, he still has a home in heaven. Unfortunately, when the question, "Where is heaven?" is asked, only vague comments like, "It is up there someplace." are given. The exact location of heaven is unknown. It is a bit disconcerting to realize that this unseen god is now in an unknown place with all these magical angels helping him out. The entire story has a fairy tale quality. Such mystical vagueness should arouse some skepticism.

On the down side, there is the concept of the devil - some sort of evil monster. He goes roaming all over the world, everywhere at the same time.

He performs much like god. But he is the epitome of evil, while god personifies goodness. The devil is out to capture people's souls.

The devil resides in hell. The location of hell is also very vague. No one seems to know where it is. Evil people end up in hell, where they live in misery for all eternity. This is a horrible, ghastly concept.

There are also some offshoots from these fundamental ideas. The immortal soul and everlasting life are additional appealing concepts. Your immortal soul (the real you), lives on after your body dies. The immortal soul of each of us is wafted off into heaven where the immortal souls live a wondrous existence for all eternity. The downside is that those who have lived evil lives will go to hell and live in torment for all eternity.

These scenarios have a fairy tale quality. There is magic involved. There are unseen beings performing mystical acts. There is an unreal tone that seems like fantasy.

The entire scenario can be thought of as a grand delusion. The definition in the dictionary of delusion is a false belief or opinion. In a psychiatric sense the dictionary definition of delusion is a false and persistent belief maintained in spite of evidence to the contrary. That last definition is a lot closer to the actual situation.

In a sense, the vast majority of the population is involved in a mental aberration - a grand delusion. Each of the believers supports the others in perpetuating the delusion. They persistently try to convert non-believers to their way of thinking, or ostracize the non-believers in order to punish them for their lack of faith. Believers do not want to change their ideas. They like believing in the delusion. They become annoyed at anyone who attempts to question their beliefs. They do not want their placid situation ruined. They want to stay deluded.

Estimates, based on public opinion surveys, indicate that about 95% of the population of the United States believe in god. The huge majority (95%) do apply a social pressure on the small minority (5%) to conform. This is a very strong, almost insidious social pressure. The faithful think of the non-believer as an atheist. To them, an atheist is somewhat sinister. An atheist is one who has no morals, nor ethics. The behavior of an atheist would be suspect. (Incidentally, the faithful do not usually think of themselves as theists.)

The fact, that an almost overwhelming percentage of the population believes in god, puts a powerful social pressure on the non-believer to join the majority. The message is to conform. Do not rock the boat!

What I will do in this book is examine these types of concepts in considerably more detail. It will be an attempt to ascertain if there is any real substance to these ideas. Is it possible to determine if there is any validity to any of these concepts? Is there a heaven and a hell? Is there such a being as god or the devil? Can conclusions be drawn from the information that is available.

If something is real, then factual information can be collected to support the concept. If something is unreal, then factual information will be totally absent. As you read this book, you will see that supporting facts are lacking for many religious ideas.

THE DEVIL YOU SAY

We are living in a highly technical, sophisticated society. Our homes and businesses are cooled by air-conditioning. Refrigerators preserve perishable foods. We drive motor vehicles at high speed over numerous highways. We wear clothing made of synthetic fibers. We watch current events, from anywhere in the world, on colored television sets. We have elaborate diagnostic tools for medical care and can partake of numerous complicated chemicals to alleviate our suffering and symptoms. We can fly on jet planes to anywhere in the world. We can use nuclear material to make devastating bombs, or to generate electrical power. Our world is, indeed, technical and awe inspiring in its complexity.

Most of these advances have been due to scientific discoveries. The application of scientific principles to everyday life has dramatically changed our society. We like to think of ourselves as "cool cats", sophisticated and worldly wise. But despite all the advances, a few things have not changed.

We cling tenaciously to some really peculiar ideas. These ideas are carry-overs from the past. These ideas did provide semi-plausible answers to questions that could not be answered in the past. These ideas did provide comfort in an uncertain world and they still do. But it is now time to examine these ideas with cold logic and try to determine if such ideas make any sense.

Religion is over-emphasized in our society and distorts almost every aspect of life. It influences how we behave, how we chose mates, how we raise our children, etc. Religion becomes a code for living.

This presents a problem, because there are so many religions, and many of them prescribe different ways of doing things. A variety of approaches to life often can conflict with each other. In extreme misunderstandings this has led to warfare between religious groups.

Even though there appear to be many beneficial aspects to religious views, they encumber their participants with somewhat rigid ways of dealing with life. Personal freedom of expression is subjugated to religious codes. Examples of these rules are: you must attend services every Sunday, you must not eat meat on Friday, you must not work on the Sabbath, women must wear a veil when in public, etc.

Unfortunately, few people examine, in detail, the validity of their religion. How did it get started? Why do we have these rules? How can we ascertain if a particular religion is correct? Who governs the organization? How valid is the governing? Etc.

Religions around the world have a host of unsubstantiated ideas. They range over the spectrum of human thought. Many people fill their mental picture of the world with mystical, magical, and even monstrous beings.

Among these ideas are the supreme being, angels, heaven, hell, and the devil. The devil is the most bizarre and certainly the most unpleasant of all the ideas.

What would you say if I told you that a beautiful, kindly, benevolent fairy princess watched over me day and night to keep me from harm. You would probably think I had gone over the deep end. And what would you think if I told you that a vicious, sinister, evil troll pursued me day and night trying to contaminate my soul. Once again, you would probably think I had gone over the deep end.

Such ideas are routinely expressed by the vast majority of people in the United States and throughout the world. These ideas are usually expressed with respect to "god" and the "devil". Stated this way, they are instantly acceptable. But should they be?

If anyone asks the question, "Is there a god?" most people will instantly resist such thinking. After all, god protects them, he cares about them, he loves them, etc. They do not want to part with the all-powerful, yet cuddlesome security-blanket up in the sky. To begin any discussion of the validity of these religious ideas with god, is barking up the wrong tree.

Instead, I want to discuss the idea of a devil. Why? Because very few people like the devil. Most people are scared to death about him. There are also a variety of names for this mythical monster. Satan and Lucifer immediately come to mind. But it makes no difference what you call this loathsome creature, he is still the epitome of evil. He is the destroyer of goodness, the moral enemy of us all.

Somehow, this monster of evil can defy the supreme master of the universe - god. This dark, foreboding, sinister figure is everywhere, spreading his agenda of misery and hate. The devil seems to be an evil god. People live in dread of this despicable being. They fear what the devil may do to them. They know that the good god is unable to control this dreadful creature. The situation is frightening.

The devil has a permanent residence - hell. All bad human beings will end up in hell. They will be at the mercy of this gruesome creature forever. What a nightmare!

Before belaboring the situation any further, it is time to ask a few penetrating questions. What evidence is there that a devil exists? Is this concept a figment of mankind's collective imagination? Where is hell? Why do people believe in such an outlandish and unwholesome thing as the devil?

The answers to these questions are clear. There is not a single shred of evidence that a devil exists. Not one fact supports this idea. The concept is strictly in the imagination of mankind. I find it difficult to understand why people would want to believe in a devil. Ugh! Who needs such an ugly concept. The same is true for hell.

Astronomers have examined billions of objects in outer space and have not located any hell. You could say that any star would be a hell hole, and that could be right . But why do we have hundreds of billions of stars in our Milky Way galaxy, and many billions of galaxies in the universe? It makes little sense. There could be hundreds, even millions of hells for each human being that ever existed. It would be overkill in the extreme.

The answer to the question, "Why do people believe in such an outlandish and unwholesome thing as a devil?" is almost certainly due to peer pressure and authoritarian edict. Most of the clergy: ministers, priests, bishops, popes, etc. say that the devil does exist. Many of your friends and family may also think so too. Therefore the devil is real. Not so!

Just because almost everyone believes in something does not make it true. The concept must be supported by facts. To believe such a far-fetched idea as the devil, a lot of facts are needed, and there are no facts to support the devil concept. The idea runs against reason. There are some insurmountable problems with the devil concept.

If there is an all-powerful master of the universe - god, why can't he control the devil? Either he can control the devil or he cannot be all-powerful. Something is amiss! And if god tolerates the devil, how can he be loving and kind? The devil counters the essence of the god figure. This is a dilemma. The entire scenario makes no sense.

Even though people wish that the devil did not exist, they cannot free themselves from the thought that he is out there somewheres. Oh how nice it would be, if the devil did not exist. (I can bring you instant relief. The devil does not exist. Think about it! You can figure it out for yourself.)

In ancient times our base of information was extremely limited compared to what it is now. People made attempts to explain a variety of happenings that they could not understand. In order to explain the bad behavior of some human beings, the concept of a devil was used. Some people lied and stole. Others battered and killed. Our primitive ancestors were not schooled in psychology and sociology, so they blamed it on the devil. "The devil made him do it." provided a neat answer for a variety of unpleasant events. All the distasteful and wrongful acts were explained with a trite phrase.

Today we know that a multiplicity of factors bring about anti-social behaviors such as: stealing and killing. It can be your upbringing, your genetic inheritance, your economic status, your choice of friends, your view of the world, your use of illegal drugs, etc. There is nothing simple about it. Simple phrases like, "The devil made him do it." Do not explain very much.

Nowadays, we have much more sensible answers to, "Why did he do it?" Some of them might be: poverty and loneliness gave him a wrong attitude, or the chemistry of his brain was not functioning properly. Anger, fear, and retaliation might also be involved. There is nothing simple about anti-social behavior. Furthermore, people are not perfect, and do make mistakes. They often cannot foresee the results of actions taken.

There are other problems with the devil concept. How can this evil being be everywhere at the same time? He must be on all sides of the earth: the northern hemisphere, the southern hemisphere, down in mines, up in airplanes, under the sea in submarines, etc. How does the devil exert his "force"? And he must be speaking in hundreds of languages at the same instant. How can the devil possibly do it? He would have to be a super being - a god. And this god must be a very bad one.

Then there is the gosh-awful problem that the good god, the supreme master of the universe is unable to control this evil god. How can the good god be the supreme master of the universe and not be able to control this evil god? It make no sense.

Either the good god is the supreme master of the universe, or he condones this evil god gadding about doing bad things. If so, then the good god cannot be as good as we hoped he would be. He allows this evil influence to ruin what would otherwise be a pleasant experience. This, indeed, is a strange behavior for an all-loving, kindly god. Something is amiss!

THE BEGINNING OF THE GOD HYPOTHESIS

In ancient times people became frightened when storms raged. The lightning flashes and the thunder crashes, and fierce winds left them with feeling of dread. They did not know what was causing the storm. A semi-plausible explanation was that a god, up in the sky, was angry. This idea persisted for many generations and almost everybody bought the idea. Nothing could satisfactorily replace the explanation that the angry god caused the storm.

But in the last two centuries there had been a growing accumulation of information about natural phenomena such as: storms, lightning flashes, floods, earthquakes, volcanoes, etc. Massive amounts of data have been collected about these happenings. There is no longer any doubt that all these events are caused by natural conditions. An angry god is not involved.

The causes of the weather, including storms, are often complex. Solar radiation, the tilt of the earth's axis, the shape of the earth's orbit about the sun, the presence of mountain ranges, the flow of oceanic currents, the turbidity of the air, and many other parameters are involved in the weather.

The weather patterns of the world are studied continuously. Satellites in outer space send back pictures of cloud formations all over the globe. Weather stations on the ground collect data on temperature, rainfall, wind velocity, etc. The weather is a perfectly natural phenomena that is understood very well.

Television forecasters can often correctly predict storms several days in advance. If a weatherman said, that the gods were angry tonight so there will be a storm, people would think the forecaster was making a joke.

Fortunately, current weather forecasting is usually fairly good The weather does follow a cause and effect process. There is no capricious maneuvering of a powerful, unseen hand to change the weather. God does not capriciously cause storms to happen. Storms are the result of natural conditions.

An interesting point could be made about this scenario. The god concept most probably began with an explanation of the weather. Yet in today's world god had been put out of a job. The accumulated facts clearly show that god does not interfere with the weather. The original beginnings of the god hypothesis has been clearly refuted. Yet the god concept marches on.

EVERLASTING LIFE

The concept of an everlasting life is a most appealing one. Everybody would like to have their existence continue, instead of ending abruptly in death. Despite the strong attractiveness of this idea, there are no facts to support it. After studying just about every known phenomena, scientific scrutiny has not come up with a single scientific fact to support such a claim. There isn't a shred of evidence that indicates everlasting life has any validity at all.

Even though most of us would earnestly want such an idea to be true., the facts are a total blank on this fervent hope. The way we would like things to be and the way things really are, all too often are on separate courses. No matter how desperately we want or wish for something, wishing and hoping does not make it so.

We all know someone who has died. We can pick up any newspaper and read about the individuals who have died in the last few days. We also know that sooner or later each one of us will end up dead. It is not too pleasant a prospect. How much nicer it would be to go to heaven and live in eternal bliss. Is such an idea fantasy or reality?

There are other aspects to heaven and everlasting life. If a loved one has died, it now becomes possible to rejoin this person in heaven. The joy of reuniting with a long lost loved one would be estatic. Instead of an irretrievable loss, the anticipation of reunion is most comforting. Death does not score the final victory. Everlasting life does! We like the idea a lot. We want to believe it.

Unfortunately, no living human being knows where heaven is. Yet when you die, you (that is your soul) unerringly finds the way to the desired location. Your soul can get there without a road map or a vehicle. How is this magic performed? Nobody knows.

Unfortunately, no one has been able to detect or contact the soul of anybody. There is little scientific information on the subject. There are no facts to support the idea of a soul and everlasting life.

All of these religious ideas are exactly what we would like to see happen. Religions often tell us what we would like to hear. They propose mystical, magical, wonders that appeal to our innermost needs.

Such a series of marvelous ideas satisfy our most intense longings. But can any of these ideas deliver what they promise? The entire series of concepts sound almost too good to be true. And I am afraid they are.

The main problem we have is to separate fantasy from reality. Fantasy is perfectly okay if we can derive pleasure and contentment from the fantasy. Be when we mix fantasy with the real situation and cannot tell which is which, then something needs to be straightened out. Real things can be contacted, examined, and measured.

Fantasy is nebulous. It is made up out of imagination. It cannot be contacted, examined, or measured. Fantasy has no real substance.

Animals, that we care for, die regularly. Most domestic animals have a much shorter life span than we do. Dogs, cats, horses, etc. disappear from the scene. In general, most people do not picture them is dog heaven, cat heaven, or horse heaven. The same sort of attitude is extended to the livestock we eat - the cows, pigs, chickens, etc. A dead animal is a dead animal. They are gone forever. Why should we be different?

From a genetic point of view, all of these animals are distant relatives of ours. Much of their DNA is very similar to ours. Some of the animal life, like the gorilla, orangutan, and chimpanzee are fairly close relatives of ours. Yet we do not consider any of them to be immortal. Just when did Homo sapiens, our human species, acquire the attribute of being immortal? And how can anyone determine such an attribute? Where is the evidence?

Furthermore, there are billions and billions of dead human beings, yet we have been unable to communicate with any of them. Despite numerous attempts to interact with the dead, such a feat has never been shown to be scientifically valid. Despite all our ardent hopes and dreams, life after death appears to be a figment of mankind's imagination. Before everlasting life can be taken seriously, there has to be some firm evidence that indicates it is real. Otherwise we are just kidding ourselves. As the old song goes, "If you wish long enough, wish strong enough, you are bound to know, that wishing will make it so." Unfortunately, wishing does not make it so. There are no facts to support the concept of everlasting life.

FAITH

The term faith is commonly used in religions. The dictionary definition of faith is a confident belief in the truth, value, or trustworthiness of a person, idea, or thing. Faith is also a belief that does not rest on logical proof or material evidence. Faith is also a belief and trust in god and the doctrines expressed in the scriptures or other sacred works.

The various definitions use belief and trust. But the belief that does not rest on logical proof or material evidence is the one that is the most bothersome. Unfortunately, almost all religious beliefs or ideas make use of that concept. Religions are based on faith that has no basis in logic or real facts. Mark Twain expressed it this way. "Faith is believing in something you know ain't true."

Various religious figures extoll the virtues of anyone whose "faith" is strong. They congratulate individuals who base their way of life on something that has no logical foundation. They eagerly endorse anyone whose uses faith as a means of settling issues.

Such behavior is the opposite of a good thinking process. Clear, rational thought processes require the use of material evidence, facts. From the facts, logical deductions can be made. But one must start from facts, not faith.

Religions insist on faith. And faith by-passes sound logical procedures. Adherents of religion are told to substitute blind belief instead of using logic. That is anti-intellectual and becomes the basis for much of religion's difficulties.

RULES ABOUT GOD

There seems to be a set of "rules" about god that most believers readily accept. There are things that god does do and doesn't do. These "rules" are mostly about what god doesn't do. On close examination these rules are baffling.

God is never seen by large groups of people, nor does god ever speak to groups of people. God never sends direct messages or explicitly conveys his desires to the people of the world. Apparently, he expresses his wishes in a few old written books, like the koran and the bible.

Apparently, it is conceded that god does appear to single individuals on extremely rare occasions. These individuals then report what god had told them. Some people also believe that god sends signs that human beings can interpret.

The rainbow after a storm was long considered by many to be a sign from god that the storm was over. Even though a rainbow is so strikingly spectacular that a magical cause for it can be readily imagined, it is not a magical phenomena. The cause of rainbows has been thoroughly studied and is well understood. A simple prism can split ordinary "white light" into the colors of the rainbow. Water droplets after a storm can do the same thing.

When someone asks, "Where is god?", they receive the answer that he is up in heaven. The directions to heaven are so vague as to be utterly meaningless. Nobody knows where heaven is and they do not know where god is either.

Nevertheless, god is supposed to be everywhere all the time. Even though he is everywhere, continuously, no one can contact him directly. He fails to communicate directly with almost everyone, almost all the time. God is most reticent.

If one examines these rules and the supposed behavior of god, they will be struck by the overall situation. God behaves exactly like an entity that does not exist. These so-called "rules" are a feeble attempt to explain away the obvious. God acts as if he were not there.

Furthermore, the stipulation that a lone individual can see or talk to god, prevents any verification of such an event. There is no possible way to determine if such an encounter is a fabrication or an illusion of the individual involved. Individual accounts of such a happening must be taken with a great deal of skepticism. All of us can image things, can dream things. That does not make them factual.

Then there are just plain liars. People who tell things in such a way that it will benefit their desires. Psychologists have learned that a great many people engage in lying. It is to be expected and should not come as a surprise.

Then there are individuals that would be classified as mentally disturbed or mentally ill. These people also have vehement ideas about a lot of unreal things. They often earnestly believe in the wild stories that they convey to others. But unfortunately, these are often without any real substance.

So god is an all-powerful, omnipresent super being who fails to convey any of this to mankind. How can we possibly know he is there if he does not make himself known? Or are we all kidding ourselves in a sort of grand delusion.

PRAYER

The idea of prayer is an old one. Primitive man did not hesitate to ask god for help. When things started to go wrong, they let the powers on high know about it. Apparently, they felt that god was so busy that he had missed some specific needs of a given individual. They wanted to let god know that they expected him to help.

They thought that by beseeching the super being to intercede, the chances of his taking appropriate action would be increased. Some primitive societies used human sacrifices to appease the gods. Even this butchery was considered to be a sort of prayer to the almighty.

So prayer has been in vogue for a very long time. What it may accomplish is difficult to ascertain. There is no firm information on which to base any conclusion. There are no scientific facts to support the idea of the "power of prayer".

However, the very idea of prayer is somewhat contradictory. If there is an all powerful, all knowing super being in charge of everything, then he certainly does not need to be prompted. He would automatically know what is best and do it, irrespective of the wishes of mere mortals.

Despite this irony, prayer is used by a great many people. They pray for loved ones to get well when they are sick. They pray to god to keep them safe when they travel, etc. Usually prayer is involved in asking the deity for something. It is a one-sided way to communicate with god. There is no way to know if he ever gets the message or if he ever took any action.

Occasionally prayer gets distorted. When sporting teams clash, one team will send up a collective prayer to the super being, asking for assistance. That of course means that the other team loses. What about the human beings on the other team? Isn't god concerned about their welfare?

In warfare the same sort of thing occurs. One side prays to god for success on the battlefield. In some cases both sides pray to god for success. How is god supposed to handle such a situation? Should he discriminate against one side against the other?

The winner of any war often claims that god was on their side and made sure they would win. There is no way to substantiate such a claim.

The overall idea of prayer accomplishing anything is dubious at best. If there is a god, he would certainly know what is going on. There is no need to grovel before him. Why should that impress him? The idea of prayer is most questionable.

It appears that the only thing that prayer has changed is the attitude of the person doing the praying. The praying person may feel soothed or uplifted by their praying action. Some intolerable situation, like a death, might become a bit more tolerable than it otherwise might be. In that sense prayer is of some psychological help. But in the real sense, praying may be an exercise in futility. If there is no master of the universe, if there is no such thing as a god, somewhere up in the sky, how can he alleviate the suffering. He may not hear the prayer because he may not exist. The prayer could fall on non-existent ears.

GOD FEARING

The term god fearing is usually used in a way that is meant to be complimentary. But when one reflects on the phrase, it is anything but complimentary. A god fearing person is one who is afraid of god. Such a person is afraid of the rage that god may invoke if anything is done "wrong".

A person who is god fearing lives a life of apprehension, treading softly, so that the all powerful god will not become irritated. Such an individual is supposedly living a good life. But what is actually occurring is that such a person is living a good life in order to avoid the wrath of god.

Avoiding the anger of god seems to be a most unworthy reason for living a good life. It is far better to live a good life because it will make you, and those about you, happy. Why devote a noble existence to fear? Why should anyone be in dread of the supreme authority? Such a distortion of the loving god should be frowned upon by believers, not admired. Calling someone a god fearing person is almost an insult.

However, the most ludicrous part of the whole idea of god fearing is that there may be no god. Apparently, some individuals spend their lives fearing something that may not exist.

PASSAGE TO HEAVEN AND HELL

There is an unusual problem presented in getting to heaven and getting to hell. Nobody knows where heaven is! Nobody knows where hell is! When we die "our soul" somehow knows exactly where it is supposed to go. How does "our soul" do that?

Somehow, the souls gets transported into heaven, if we have been good people during our lives. And on the down side, if we have been bad, sinful people we get transported into hell. How this is accomplished in most unclear!

Is there a bus that leaves every hour? And if there is, it better be a very big bus. Thousands of people die every hour. And these people are scattered all over the globe. When one person is dying in Peru, another is exiting in India, Kenya, and Bermuda. The next moment it could be China, France, Mexico, and Chile. The dying goes on endlessly.

Nearly six billion people are alive today and very few live to be over 100 years old. If we assume that the average life span is about 60 years, then about 100 million people die every year. There are about 30 million seconds in a year. That means that about 3 people die every second, about 200 every minute, and about 12,000 every hour.

The logistics of sorting and transporting all these individuals into heaven and hell would be a crushing task. And it goes on continuously, night and day, all over the globe. It make one wonder how it can be accomplished, or if it can be accomplished.

How can the devil or god know when and where each and every one of these thousands will expire? How can they possibly keep track of them all? How can they be all over the planet from one second to the next? How can they transport all these souls into heaven or into hell? And where the heck are heaven and hell anyway?

That is a lot of unanswered questions. The entire operation sounds too complicated, too magical, to possibly be true. The unseen god and the unseen devil are magically whisked hither and yon all over the planet continuously. That is in addition to their routine tasks of paying attention to everyone and everything in the entire world. The combined tasks defy the imagination. The entire scenario reads like a fairy tale and not a very good one.

A skeptical view of this entire scenario is justified. And last but not least, there is not a single scientific fact that indicates any of these actions occur. They appear to be fantasies.

GOD AND PUNISHMENT

The idea that god would punish individuals for their misdeeds is all too common. A great many people believe that if something dreadful happens to a person, it is the punishment of god. They unconsciously condemn a person if something goes wrong.

This distorted bias creates a host of difficulties. A person with a problem finds himself or herself being shunned or avoided by former friends.

An example of such a situation is the following. A baby is born with a severe birth defect. The grandmother of the newborn scathingly inquiries of her daughter, the mother, with the phrase, "What despicable deeds you must have done that god would punish you like this." An extremely stressful situation degenerates into something much worse. Instead of the support, that the mother desperately needs, she is confronted with hostility.

If we take this particular example of a birth defect, and then examine the validity of the accusation, we might be able to determine something about the possible punishment of god.

Scientific information indicates that birth defects are caused by a variety of factors. Among the many causative factors are various diseases, genetic abnormalities, and an assortment of chemical agents.

Some diseases that cause birth defects are contracted in a normal living situation. A given individual has little control over the exposure. Genetic defects are inherited from ancestors, and an individual has no control over his or her parentage. The same sort of situation applies to chemical agents. All too often a given individual is totally unaware that he or she has been exposed. Usually there is no firm connection between the behavior of parents and birth defects.

However, there can be a connection between birth defects and parental behavior. If the parents had used alcohol, drugs, or smoked cigarettes, then various chemicals in these materials can have deleterious effects on the offspring.

Even so, there is no indication that god interferes in the process. The causative agents are specific chemicals and their effects have been studied. Their cause and effect relationship are known. There is no need for any god to participate in order to bring about birth defects.

But let us suppose that god did such a monstrous deed - produce a baby with a severe birth defect. Certainly the parents will suffer, but what of the totally innocent child? The child is condemned to a life of misery. What sort of a god would do such a dastardly thing as bring forth a defective baby to punish a parent. It makes little sense.

RELIGIOUS BELIEFS IN GENERAL

The chief reason for the proliferation of religions around the world is that there is no decisive way to show the truth or falsehood of many religious ideas. Few of these diverse ideas are supported by firm facts. Most of these religious ideas are in the realm of abstract thought.

Before proceeding further, the concept of a scientific fact must be thoroughly explained. A scientific fact is some measurement or observation that can be repeated or supported by numerous scientific workers. A single individual making a claim is insufficient for establishing a scientific fact. Additional support or evidence from others must be obtained before the fact can be established. One person making a claim does not constitute a scientific fact.

Two scientific facts are: the boiling point of water (which is 100 degrees Celcius when the atmospheric pressure is 760 torr), and that salmon leave the ocean and go up fresh water streams to spawn. Both of these facts have been determined by numerous workers making the measurement or observation. Anyone can check the validity of both of these facts by repeating the measurement or observation themselves. When the statement is made in this book that scientific facts support or do not support a specific concept, these are the type of facts under consideration.

If we examine some of the religious concepts, the statements are often too tenuous to evaluate.

Some examples follow: (1) "Mary the mother of god, was a virgin." (2) "The angel Gabriel is up in heaven." (3) God is made up of three persons, the father, the son, and the holy ghost."

It is essentially impossible to show that any of these concepts are correct. Any attempt to determine the virginity of someone who has been dead for about 2,000 years is asking too much. Furthermore, there is no body to examine. Determining the validity of such a statement is not possible.

The second statement involves heaven. No one knows where heaven is, much less if a given entity resides in this location. The validity of such a statement cannot be determined.

The third statement involves three subdivisions of god. This does present a problem. How can we examine god when direct communication with god is not possible? How can anyone tell what god is composed of? Why is god split into three pieces? There is no way to conduct an examination, no way to ascertain the validity of such a statement.

The fundamental validity of statements or concepts of this type defies any rational method of analysis. Stated bluntly, there is no way to positively show if these statements or concepts are pure fantasy or really valid ideas.

The situation is so bizarre. Numerous religious statements are made and there is no information to indicate that these concepts are valid. Without any facts to support such statements, they have to fall into the category of pure speculation. Abstract thinking unsupported by any evidence.

Lets go back to the first statement, "Mary the mother of god, was a virgin." From a scientific point of view, a virgin female can only become pregnant when a human male sperm contacts a human female egg. Nowadays, a woman can be artificially inseminated without engaging in the sex act. But about 2,000 years ago, such procedures were not available.

The big question is, "Why does it matter if Mary was a virgin or not?" The inference is that there is something wrong or degrading about engaging in sex. The birth of Christ must be immaculate, and free from any contamination of normal, necessary human acts of reproduction. The sex act is portrayed as dirty or unclean. This sort of religious bias permeates so much of our culture. And these biases often are based on statements that defy validation.

Chapter 2

IMPLICATIONS ABOUT THE GOD HYPOTHESIS

VARIATIONS OF THE GOD HYPOTHESIS

Santa Claus is an obvious variation of the god hypothesis. Santa is a magical figure that signifies kindness and concern for children. He appears for one day of the year, Christmas, and makes children happy by giving them gifts. He, somehow, is supposed to watch over the children and determine if they have been bad or good. Their gifts from Santa supposedly reflect their good or bad behavior throughout the year.

Most adults have little difficulty with the Santa Claus hypothesis. They know it is a fairy tale. The jolly old elf, Santa, is a make believe person. Even though we can actually see Santa in various department stores, we know that no real Santa exists.

Rather than asking the question, "Is there a Santa Claus?", asking "Who is Santa Claus?" provides a means of determining an answer. A fairly simple mathematical approach to that question is informative.

Two sets of facts are needed to begin - the population of the United States and the number of seconds in a year. The population of the United States is about 250 million persons. About 4 individuals live in an average home, so that about 60 million homes exist. The number of seconds in a year are 31,536,000, or about 30 million.

(Do not worry about the rounding off of numbers being too extreme. We are just trying to establish an order of magnitude rather than a mathematically exact answer.)

If Santa is given one second in which to visit each home in the United States, it would take him about 2 full years of continuous labor to visit all 60 million homes in the country. Furthermore there would be no time for travel between homes. The chance for one individual to get the job done on Christmas is totally impossible.

Two years represents about 700 days. Santa operates in the darkness of Christmas, about a 12 hour period. If 1,400 persons acted as Santa they could visit each home in the 12 hours of darkness, assuming one second per home. Once again, there is no time allowed for travel between homes.

A more realistic approach would be to allow one minute for each home visit. This would mean that 80,000 Santas would be required to visit each home in the 12 hour period of darkness. The problem of travel between homes has not be considered.

If a one hour per visit is allowed then about 5 million Santas would be needed to visit every home in the United States on Christmas eve, The one hour would allow some time for travel between various homes.

So we can conclude that millions of Santas would be needed. Santa Claus must be a fairly high percentage of the total population. And that means that Santa Claus is us!

Santa Claus is not a magical figure sledding around the wintry countryside. Santa Claus is all the people: the parents, grandparents, friends, etc. who are concerned about the welfare of children. They make the "magic" of Christmas happen.

Superman is another mystical being that has attributes that border close to those of god. Superman is against evil and crime. He can perform prodigious feats of strength. He can fly through the air faster than a speeding bullet. Superman does good deeds.

Despite the close approximation to the god figure, practically no one confuses the comic strip character with god. Almost everyone agrees that superman is a make believe person - a figment of the human imagination.

There are some practical reasons for questioning the validity of the superman concept. Superman performs real feats. Flying rapidly through the air is one such feat. How does he do it? How can anyone fly without some mechanical help like an airplane or a helicopter? What provides the energy for such flight?

In the comic strip, superman just wills it. But everyone knows that an object can only be moved by exerting a force. And energy is required to exert a force. That is a fundamental principle of physics. The idea of superman fails to be convincing because he is supposed to perform real deeds - things that can be readily evaluated.

Such variations of the god hypothesis are relatively easily exposed as fantasy. The big question is, "Why doesn't the god hypothesis collapse the same way?" The god concept does not have any more going for it than Santa Claus or superman. The god hypothesis is just a more elaborate and traditional concept that has been accepted in the past. Now we have the tradition of our culture that expects us to believe the magical tale.

But the most important aspect should not be lost. People like to believe the god hypothesis. They do not want to lose the "protection" it affords. Even though the god hypothesis does not actually give any protection, people want to believe that it does. They do not want to be exposed to the vicissitudes of life. They want to hide behind a protector - a shield. The god concept seems to furnish this so-called protection. But it may be an illusion.

WORLD RELIGIONS

The vast assortment of religions around the world is truly astonishing. The wide diversity almost defies description. Some of the major groupings are: Buddist, Christian, Hebrew, Hindu, Moslem, etc.

Most of these major groups can be subdivided further. The Christian religion is split into numerous sects. A few are: Roman Catholic, Episcopalian, Lutheran, Baptist, Methodist, Mormon, Amish, etc. The Christian religions, by themselves are a "Tower of Babel". When the numerous subdivisions of all the other religions are included, the overall religious picture becomes almost chaotic.

Why are there so many different religious subdivisions? How could such a confused arrangement develop?

It appears that religious concepts are totally out of control. Down through the ages, new religions have been formed as new concepts were visualized by various religious leaders. No cohesive force seemed to be guiding them. The religious leaders just tried to convince everyone that they had the right idea. But with time, the number of dissenters kept growing. So did the list of religions.

But the most intriguing part of this entire scenario is that each and every one of these subdivisions is SURE that they and only they have the correct approach. Each subdivision is absolutely certain that they are right. They grudgingly tolerate the others as misguided souls who do not know any better.

Ask the question, "Can all these different religions be correct?" A little thought will clearly indicate that all these various approaches cannot be correct. There is no way all can be on target. From a mathematical point of view, the best that can be expected is that one of them might be correct. Although the distinct possibility exists that none of them are correct.

For the moment, let's assume the most favorable possibility, that one is correct. What does that tell us? It tells us that god, the total master of the universe, has allowed a jumble of religious ideas to develop. Even if the most popular religion in the world is the correct one, that leaves the vast majority of humanity following some wrong approach.

Why does the supreme ruler of the universe let so many of his devout followers take the wrong path? These people all want to do the right thing. Why are they not given some hint of the correct route to follow? It is baffling to try to understand why the vast majority of believers must be doing the wrong thing. Why would god let so many of his people go astray? It is most perplexing!

We are left scratching our heads. There does not seem to be any logical explanation for the chaotic religious situation of today's world. So let's try another look.

If there is no god to oversee the situation, the wide diversity is easy to explain. All of these religions are due to the whims and ideas of numerous human beings, down through the centuries. The information available about human behavior, and the wide assortment of human cultures around the world, indicate that a diverse assortment of religions should be expected.

In various environments around the world, different languages are spoken, different foods are eaten, different structures are built, etc. The diversity of human cultures is broad. We should expect that ideas about a deity should also be different.

Without any god to steer them, the various peoples of the world went their merry way. They took various approaches. No firm guidelines directed them to take a specific path. They did pretty much what their religious leaders told them to do.

Atrocities of the worst kind were performed as religious rites. Some ancient religions practiced human sacrifices. Some of these gruesome practices still persist in some of today's religions. Female genital mutilation, the so-called female circumcision, is still part of the religious rites of some groups today. It is performed, without anesthetics on young girls before they reach puberty.

Despite its claim to religious rite, the practice is bestial and barbaric. Yet those who practice it feel it is their god-given right to do this despicable deed. Female genital mutilation must be stopped!

The development of the various religions has been uneven. Protesters of various dogma have split off and established their own religion. As time goes on, more and more subdivisions appear. There does not seem to be any cure for the proliferation of religions.

Examining the world religious situation is disconcerting. Everyone seems to think that everyone else is wrong. Yet no one agrees that they are wrong. How can anyone determine the validity of the ideas that are incorporated in these various religions? Obviously, such a determination is not easy.

Rather than meticulously examining each and every claim, it might be more productive to try to ascertain the validity of the major premise - the idea of god being in charge. If this fundamental idea is false, then the subsequent ideas based on it are likewise false. Wrong ideas beget more wrong ideas. So to end it, the original wrong idea must be eliminated.

Whether we like it or not, there are a great many indicators that god does not exist! When the assumption is made that god does exist, it leads to all kinds of mischief.

THE CHURCHES OF TODAY

Churches serve a useful function. Each church is a social group, a sort of extended family relationship to the members. The interest and support of the church group provides a much needed warmth and closeness that is not available elsewhere. People like this type of togetherness. They will resist losing such an association.

However, there is an unfavorable side to this social organization. The cement that holds the church social group together is the shared allegiance to some religious creed. This tends to screen out almost everyone else. The church social group becomes a restricted, almost exclusive club. Anyone, who is not in close agreement with their religious beliefs, is eliminated from participation. The church organization becomes a wedge, that tends to drive the various religious groups apart.

In some cases, the wedge becomes a very deep division. Marriages are a good example of a problem presented by religions. A Catholic would hesitate to marry a non-Catholic. Even similar religious sects present some difficulties. A Lutheran might have misgivings about a future spouse who is a Baptist. And an Episcopalian would have considerable difficulty in accommodating the ideas or a Mormon or a Jehovah's Witness.

The Amish remain almost exclusive to their own religious group in choosing a mate. So do members of the Hebrew faith. Their religious beliefs dominate their selection of a marriage partner. Their religion provides a barrier to normal human interaction.

There can be no doubt that religious groups provide a means of driving people apart. Religious ideas become a gulf between people. There are so many religious ideas, that clashes in ideas are commonplace. Religions provide a means of promoting animosity between groups. Religious differences have been the fuel that has fed the fires of many wars. In the past, the crusades were an outstanding example of religious warfare. Recently, Protestants have been allied again Catholics, Muslims against Jews, Sunni Muslims against Shiite Muslims, Christian Serbs against Bosnian Muslims, etc. It is truly a sad situation.

Despite the good wishes of many religious people, the end result of religion is the fragmentation of the human condition. Religious differences are artificial barriers between people. This separation is brought about by the incorrect thinking of human beings. They think thoughts that are unreal and then try to use them in the real world. It presents problems.

Many of these religious ideas must be changed, if humankind is ever to achieve peace on earth. The all too common fanatical, immovable stance of religious zealots leads to hostile confrontations. Religious ideas invite hostile attitudes and disputes. Religious groups are routinely squabbling among themselves. Such dissent causes a further and further fragmentation of the religions of the world.

I am aware that the world's organized religions will not fade away overnight. But religious groups should shift their emphasis. Instead of concentrating on god and doing things to please god, they should emphasize the brotherhood of man. Religious objectives should not be to adore god, but to achieve peace and harmony among all men on earth. Religions should focus on the human issues. They really need attention.

Our everyday world is filled with problems. We have earthquakes, hurricanes, tornadoes, storms, droughts, floods, etc. We also have wars, diseases, starvation, plagues, pollution, etc. The big protector in the sky seems to have lost track of a lot of the troubles of the world. You might almost think that he is not doing his job very well, if at all.

Much of the religious ritual is mumbo-jumbo nonsense. Such pointless ritual should be discarded and replaced with a much needed leadership on social problems. The sooner organized religions realize they are on the wrong track the better. But I would hate to hold my breath until they do change. I am afraid it might take centuries to accomplish such a feat.

Religions are not providing the leadership and action that is desperately needed in today's world. They are focusing on irrelevant and wrong ideas. As long as they cling to the basically incorrect ideas about god, they will remain on the sidelines. Unfortunately, it looks like the organized religions will continue to flounder down the hopeless path they have been treading.

GOD IS MENTIONED EVERYWHERE

For believers, the concept of god is expressed repeatedly. This relentless reference to god is made on many significant occasions. The religious litany bombards almost everyone who attends gatherings of people.

In many homes and groups every meal is started with a prayer of thanks to god for the food on the table. Heads are usually bowed in deference to the almighty provider. But actually, god had nothing to do with bringing food to the table. People did it. The wrong entity is being thanked. God has never been seen plowing a field, or picking fruit, nor did he drive a delivery truck to the super market. A lot of people are responsible for bringing food to the table, but god is not.

At many civic meetings, the proceedings are often begun with a prayer for guidance. A chaplain, or some other religious person, asks for the blessing of god on the group and their undertaking. There is never any sign that god hears or responds to these supplications. Yet the prayers continue nevertheless.

There is supposed to be a separation of church and state, yet public officials do not hesitate to show that they are on the side of god. All too often, high officials, like the president and governors, beseech the blessings of god on the people or the country. "God bless America" is a favorite phrase.

This repetitious reinforcement that god is real is a difficult thing to overcome. The evidence, that people think there is a god, is everywhere. Churches, of all sorts of denominations, dot the countryside. The church spires can be seen for miles. Our money uses the term, "In god we trust". The concept of god as reality, is accepted by so many people that it is difficult to ignore. Any individual is almost coerced into believing that god does exist. To think that god does not exist is out of step with almost everyone else.

Anyone, who wishes to rid themselves of the concept of god, has a lot of work to do. Overturning ideas, that have been pounded into your thoughts since the beginning of your existence, takes time. But think about it a lot. Ask yourself about the value of a god who may not be there.

Any time god is mentioned by anyone, for any reason, ask some skeptical questions. For example, when the president says, "God bless America", what does it mean. How does god go about blessing America? Is the good weather the blessing of god? Then there is all that bad weather - the hurricanes, tornadoes, flash floods, etc. Is that the blessing of god? If so, why does god do so many contradictory things? Are any of these god's blessing? How can you tell?

The phrase, "In god we trust" on our paper money is baffling. What do we trust god to do? And does god do it or someone else? How can anyone determine if the action of god is responsible?

One of the pat answers, for perplexing situations involving the god idea, is the statement, "God moves in mysterious ways". I'll say he does. He moves just like he is not there!

Being skeptical is essential for shaking the smothering cloak of protection, supposedly provided by god, that really may not be there. Actually, you have nothing to lose by realizing that god may not exist.

THE HABIT OF IRRATIONAL THOUGHT

One of the by-products of believing in god is that it could put into motion a chain of irrational thinking. People really believe that god will see to it that justice will triumph and that the right thing will be done eventually. People expect god to protect them. People expect god to do a lot of things. Unfortunately, if there is no god, he will be unable to do anything. So people go about believing in some sort of mystical magic that will save them from disasters. When the magic does not occur, they appear confused and betrayed. Where was god when they needed him most?

If the god concept is an invalid hypothesis, then everything that springs from the god hypothesis could be tainted. People who lean heavily on the god concept often produce faulty thinking on a variety of topics.

The diverse assortment of religions around the world is probably the most obvious result of this questionable god hypothesis. The conflicts and animosity generated by these diverse religious ideas are a bane on humankind at both the personal and national level.

The fundamental idea that there is a big protector up in the sky could be wrong. Anyone, who truly believes that such a god is real, behaves and thinks differently than one who does not. The believer of god interprets the hand of god in almost everything. The food on the table, the pleasant day, the singing birds, their own good health, etc. are all interpreted as the handiwork of god. God becomes responsible for everything.

Every ant and every mosquito are viewed as made by god. (I suspect that some people are reluctant to swat a mosquito because they do not want to destroy the handiwork of god.) The god hypothesis has far reaching effects on the daily thought processes of many people.

Such faulty thinking is evident on the prayer of thanks before eating a meal. God is thanked reverently for placing food on the table. But the thanks are directed to the wrong source. It would be far more reasonable to thank the farmers, ranchers, truckers, grocers, chemists, biologists, etc. for the efforts expended by these human beings to bring food to the table. Food arrives on the table because of the efforts of a great many people, including the cook. God had nothing to do with it.

Ideas like this can be illustrated with a little story. The pastor of a church had permitted a hard luck parishioner to work a plot of land fairly close to the church, so that vegetables could be grown to help feed the family.

In the early fall, the pastor looked over the bountiful harvest and was impressed. He said to the man, "It is amazing what you and the lord have accomplished with this small plot of land." The man replied, "You should have seen what it was like when the lord was taking care of it all by himself."

Irrational thinking is undesirable from a personal point of view, but it becomes a social driving force when entire groups follow irrational thought processes. On the international front, religious bias is often an integral part of the tensions between nations.

Religious differences generate national animosity. Throughout history wars have been fought for god. This is carrying irrational thinking to the extreme.

Irrational wars based on religion are still occurring. Religion is usually not the only difference of opinion, but religion seems to provide a rallying point for the opposing sides. Jews have been fighting Moslems in the middle east for decades. In Pakistan and India, Moslems and Hindus have been engaged in bloody conflicts for decades. In Lebanon there is a multifaceted religious conflict. Christians fight Moslems, Jews fight Moslems, and Moslems factions quarrel among themselves. In Bosnia there is bitter animosity between Christians and Moslems.

Even though the differences are considerably broader than religion, the religious bias embitters and aggravates the problems. The religious differences make animosity easier to perpetuate.

All of this hostility is not the primary aim of religions. The avowed purpose of most religions is to provide a code of ethics, a way of life that is harmonious with nature and with fellow human beings. All too often religious differences tend to achieve almost the exact opposite.

Religions have failed rather miserably in trying to reach their goal of peace and harmony in the world. The reason for their failure is not clear, but I suspect that the problem is fundamental. Religions are working from a wrong hypothesis. They think there is a god running things. And there probably isn't.

Religions can be compared to engineers constructing a building. If any magnificent structure is built on loose sand, the building will have serious problems. Its very foundation is insecure. First and foremost in building construction is the basic need for a stable and secure foundation. Without a firm foundation the resulting structure will undergo all sorts of difficulties.

Religions need a stable foundation too. But they start out with the god hypothesis. That is their fundamental concept. That is their base. No wonder they are having troubles.

THE DESTRUCTION OF CHURCHES

Occasionally a church gets destroyed by some natural occurrence such as: a lightning bolt, a tornado, or an earthquake. When such a catastrophe occurs to a church, there is a certain amount of consternation by the members of the parish. They wonder about the reasons for such a dismal turn of events. They might find it difficult to understand how god could let their church get ruined. They consider the church to be god's church, and he let it be destroyed. Why didn't god do something to save the church?

Religious officials use a variety of flimsy excuses for the failure of the deity to protect his own property. They may state that it is a testing time and that god is letting nature take its course to see how well the faithful can recover from the ordeal. They may also use the outworn phrase, that god moves in mysterious ways.

It seems downright implausible that any god would allow the outright destruction of his own establishment. It simply would not happen if god were in charge. However, if there is no god, then the church must take its chances with the vicissitudes of nature, just like any other structure. A church would not be protected from destruction by a god who is not there. A church could become the victim of natural disasters.

Unfortunately, churches do fall victims to natural disasters and at about the same rate as other structures. Churches receive no special protection.

In the destruction of churches, if there is a god, he behaves just like he is not there.

THE HOLOCAUST

The genocide, perpetrated by Nazi Germany on the Jews in Europe during World War II, is the most ghastly and extensive series of crimes ever committed by the human race. Humankind has performed many dastardly deeds, but this organized butchery was the worst series of atrocities that ever occurred.

Members of the Jewish community were trapped in Europe by the invading German armies. They had no way to escape. The Jews were herded into concentration camps and systematically killed. The degradation and misery these people suffered at the hands of their captors was indescribably hideous.

Throughout this series of outrages, that continued for years, the Jews prayed for god to save them. They had no where else to turn. The situation was truly hopeless. Yet, despite their numerous pleas to heaven, they perished by the millions. The carnage was finally stopped after the Allied forces had stormed across Nazi Germany and captured the concentration camps.

Within the concentration camps were found starved people, barely clinging to life. The gas chambers and mass crematoriums were there for everyone to see. The horror was almost beyond belief. Nothing so repulsive and despicable had ever been know to occur before. The desperate prayers of the millions of victims had fallen on deaf ears. God did not spare them their prolonged agony. No action was taken to alleviate their suffering. Millions went to their deaths. Their last and only hope, god, had failed to do anything.

What kind of a god would do such a thing? What could be the purpose of so much suffering and death? What sort of love did god show to all these victims? How could a just and loving god tolerate such bestial behavior for so many years?

The concept of a loving god, who watches over us and protects us, loses all meaning when the holocaust is examined. Any attempt to try to understand this ghastly situation mires in confusion, if not outright despair. The god hypothesis fails to account for the holocaust. It fails badly.

If one uses the approach that there is no god, then the entire situation can be explained easily. The Nazis were in complete control of most of Europe. They could do exactly what they wanted to do. And they wanted to kill all the Jews they could get their hands on. So they did.

They believed there was no god to stop them. They behaved as though no god existed. Everyone who was in their power, that they wanted dead, was killed. No heavenly power made the slightest move to stop them.

Eventually they were stopped. But it was not by any heavenly force. The brute force of the Allied armies destroyed the German armies in vicious, open warfare. Numerous bloody battles were fought to overpower the Nazis. Many thousands of combatants died on both sides during the struggle.

Apparently, the side of justice finally triumphed But human methods were needed to bring it about. The forces of heaven were nowhere to be found. The final victory was a combination of: superior weapons, greater resources, better organization, individual courage, etc. Human efforts finally stopped the carnage of the holocaust. The entire situation can be explained without resorting to any supernatural actions. People, just people, account for it all.

An after thought is worth considering. Who would want a god that would let such a miserable series of grisly events occur on such a massive scale for so long.

HUMAN DISASTERS

Throughout history, humankind has suffered a series of disasters. These have involved volcanic eruptions, earthquakes, floods, and disease. One disaster was Pompeii in ancient Rome. Several communities were totally wiped out in the volcanic eruptions. History notes numerous similar episodes.

In the last century, there have been some devastating disasters. In central China there was a massive earthquake that killed hundreds of thousands of human beings. In Bangladesh, there was a typhoon that killed about one million people. The list of major disasters in this past century is large.

Volcanic eruptions, earthquakes, and severe weather are all too common. Humankind is beginning to cope with these disasters slightly better in recent years, but the damage is still profound. This almost incessant series of natural disasters, that keep occurring all over the world, are troublesome.

When an overall look at the disasters is made, it is baffling in the extreme. What can possibly be the purpose of killing such a massive number of human beings? If there is a god why doesn't he do something to stop it? How are individual persons going to avoid such disasters?

As near as anyone can tell, god does not initiate such events. And it is also very obvious that he does not stop them from occurring.

But natural disasters are only a small part of the catastrophes that continue to plague humankind. Diseases have decimated the human population on many occasions. Europe was devastated by the black death during the middle ages.

In North America, the introduction of smallpox by the Europeans decimated the native Indian population shortly after Columbus discovered America. Malaria has been, and still is, a devastating disease that kills millions of people every year. Currently, the AIDS epidemic is slowly sweeping across the world and will end up killing millions of people.

Diseases of various kinds have taken a terrific toll of human beings down through the centuries. There is every indication that god had nothing to do with the onset of these diseases. But on the other hand he obviously did nothing to bring such calamities to an end.

And last, but certainly not the least, are the wars that have stressed humankind ever since civilization began. Human beings have been diligently engaged in slaughtering each other for thousands of years. They are still doing it today.

Fortunately, some progress has been made, lately, in lessening the mayhem. But warfare is brutal. World War I brought death to millions. Then World War II brought death to even more. That war ended in the killing of about 200,000 persons in the cities of Hiroshima and Nagasaki with the explosion of atomic bombs.

The toll of warfare has been savage and extensive. Not only have military personnel died, but an extremely large number of civilians, including millions of children, have perished as well. Where was god through all these centuries of warfare? Where was god this century? How can a merciful god let such debacles occur? If there is a god, he acts just like he is not there.

OVERALL SUMMARY OF THE RELIGIOUS SITUATION

The overall summary of the religious situation is truly bothersome. The vast majority of humankind is going about their lives assuming something is valid when it may be completely false. The best way to describe this bizarre situation is to call it the Grand Delusion.

The vast majority of humankind believes in something that has no supporting evidence. Such a belief is an aberration of clear thinking. False ideas can certainly interfere with any rational decision process.

The Grand Delusion encompasses most of humankind. The vast majority believe in god - a benevolent, caring god. They focus a lot of their attention on this concept. They consider what god would want. They try to please god, to be good people. Such considerations permeate almost everything believers do. The god hypothesis is one of the dominant features of their everyday life. There is no question that the Grand Delusion - the collective belief that there is a god - does impinge on many aspects of our modern lives. In essence, humankind is not only deceiving itself, but is suffering a collective mental disorder.

We have to ask ourselves, "Why does the idea of god persist?" The answer to this question involves the hopes and fears of individual human beings.

The idea of a god is so comfortable, so reassuring, it is what we all want. The idea of a big, all-powerful, all-knowing protector in the sky is so appealing, so shielding, that it is almost irresistible. No wonder people, cling to the idea with such tenacity. They want to believe!

All of us wish for things. We want to live forever. We want to be safe and secure. We want to be shielded from the arbitrary disasters of life that seem to overtake so many of our fellow human beings. The god hypothesis and its associated ideas seem to give us what we want. But they only seem to give us these things. Believing has changed nothing, except our perception of the situation. And that perception may be false. Wrong ideas can lead to all sorts of mischief.

The words of an old song tend to explain it. "If you wish strong enough, wish long enough, you are bound to know, that wishing will make it so." Unfortunately, the words of the song are wrong. No matter how hard we wish, wishing does not make it so. What we wish for, and the way things really are, are often far apart.

The demands and problems of our modern world are difficult and complex. Over-population, world-wide pollution, the dangers of nuclear war, etc. are so challenging that solving them will take the very best thinking by almost everyone, to overcome them. If humankind continues to assume that god will help solve these problems, then humankind will continue to move in wrong directions. We must start from a true, logical base in order to reach realistic, conclusions.

The age old wishful thinking of religions has got to go. Fuzzy thinking has no place in our complex world-wide society. Religious ideas are all too often illogical because they are based on what may be irrational thinking - believing that a god exists. Instead, the world needs good sense and clear judgment.

The Grand Delusion, that there is a god, should not be accepted so readily in the modern world. We have got to stop collectively deceiving ourselves.

Can religions deliver on the promises they make? Or are all those concepts empty promises.

Perhaps the phrase, "If it sounds too good to be true, it probably is." And let's face it. Religions convey a picture that is so magical, so wondrous, and pleasant that it should arouse skepticism. Religions convey a picture that does, indeed, look too good to be true.

Chapter 3

SCENCE AND RELIGION

THE ORIGIN OF LIFE

Most religious people believe that life requires a supernatural being - a god. They seem to believe that life is so complex and wonderful that only a deity could ever make it happen. Perhaps this idea might have been plausible a century ago, but today a vast accumulation of scientific facts indicate the hand of a magical god is not needed to bring life to the earth.

The first significant experiment in the origin of life took place about forty years ago. A gaseous mixture composed of: hydrogen, methane, ammonia, and water was subjected to a reoccurring electrical discharge. The gaseous mixture was assumed to be similar to the original atmosphere of the earth. After several days of sparking, the resulting mixture was analyzed.

To almost everyone's astonishment, some of the major products were biochemicals. For example: glycine is the most common amino acid found in the life system on earth. Alanine is the second most common amino acid. Within the mixture, formed from the original hydrogen, methane, ammonia, and water were both glycine and alanine. Furthermore, glycine was the most abundant amino acid formed in the mixture, and alanine was the second most abundant. The experiment was an astounding success and opened the door to further research in the origin of life.

Since then, a large number of additional experiments have been made about the origin of life. All of the essential biochemicals of the life system have been studied. The most interesting feature is that these somewhat complex biochemicals have formed spontaneously under conditions that prevailed on the primitive earth about 4 billion years ago.

The vast majority of life on earth is made up mostly of about fifty simple molecules. Laboratory experiments have decisively demonstrated that these essential compounds all form readily under a wide assortment of crude conditions.

Additional experiments have demonstrated that some of these molecules form aggregates that are capable of self-replication. And self-replication is one of the main features of life. Further work has demonstrated that simple molecules can clump together to form polymeric units, much as amino acids clump together to form protein in the life system. Many organic molecules have been shown to easily form cell-like structures.

However, what is probably the most decisive part of this work is that nothing has been discovered that would block the spontaneous formation of life from relatively common molecules. On the contrary, most of the work indicates that life could have arisen under naturally occurring conditions on the primitive earth.

One of the major attributes of life is that it is self-replicating. What this indicates is that when a suitable molecular arrangement formed, then the process could continue, because the molecular arrangement would be self-replicating.

The primitive oceans of the world were a complex solution of biochemicals and other molecules, a sort of primordial soup. Once the self-replicating first molecular arrangement formed, it could reconstruct itself over and over again from the ingredients in the primitive ocean.

Furthermore, once the first primitive form of life appeared, the slow and painstaking process of evolution could take over. Gradually, through the millions and billions of years that life has existed on earth, life progressed and became more sophisticated, culminating in our modern biota.

All of the many forms of life found on the earth today developed from one ancestral form. No magic or miracles was required. The concept of the origin of life is compatible with all the known natural laws of chemistry, physics, and mathematics. Every step is in agreement with scientific information.

The origin of life concept is supported by fossils found in rocks all over the earth. The fossil record begins with primitive one celled organisms in rocks that are 3.5 billion years old. The fossil record has been followed up to today.

The fossil record shows that life relentlessly persisted, and gradually changed. The overall picture that the fossils tell us is that life tended to become more sophisticated and diverse as time went on. All of life gradually became changed and produced an assortment of life forms. Some were successful and persisted for millions of years.

Others were on the stage of life for brief periods, then became extinct.

But the overall trend was there. As time went on, life became more sophisticated. The first known macro-forms of life, appeared about 600 million years ago. The first primitive mammals about 70 million years ago. The first modern man, Homo sapiens sapiens, about 50 thousand years ago.

Nothing known to science refutes the origin of life by natural processes. There is every reason to believe that is how it happened. Miracles from a divine being are not required. Although the entire scenario is not completely known, and probably never will be known, it is reasonable to conclude that life began spontaneously following natural processes.

Despite the clear and massive scientific evidence supporting the origin of life by natural processes, many religious people do not change their position. Their ideas, based on faith, persist. I suppose this approach would be tolerable if they kept their mistaken ideas to themselves. But many religious people are trying to force their mistaken ideas about the origin of life and of evolution onto everyone else. The intense passion of their religious ideas does not change the scientific facts. The scientific facts indicate that they are wrong.

SHOWING SOMETHING EXISTS

If something exists it is usually relatively simple to demonstrate that fact. You just show the item. It is easy to show that a sparrow or an oak tree exists. Both of these items are common in many parts of the world.

But can we prove the existence of an elephant. That is not as easy, but it certainly is not difficult. All that is necessary is to go to a zoo or a circus where elephants are routinely kept.

Showing that a whale exists is a bit more difficult. Although some aquatic parks may have a whale on display, a trip to the ocean might be required. Then a tour of areas of the ocean where whales are routinely found might be arranged. Nevertheless, the reality of a whale can be demonstrated. If something exists, it is usually fairly easy to demonstrate that fact.

That brings up a most important point. If you cannot demonstrate that something does exist, does that mean that it does not exist? Not necessarily! The very fact that evidence cannot be found for the existence of something is somewhat compelling, but not absolutely certain. Or restating the situation, if something exists it is usually relatively easy to demonstrate the reality of its existence. But to demonstrate that something does not exist is extremely difficult.

About the best that can be done is to conclude that something does not exist, if there is no evidence that it does exist. However, there is always the remote possibility that evidence of such existence might be discovered. Nevertheless, it is far more reasonable to conclude that something does not exist, if nothing indicates it does exist.

In order to overthrow a conclusion that something does not exist, facts are required. Even one decisive fact would suffice. But without any facts, the conclusion of non-existence will remain reasonable.

Let's look at an example. Do mammoths exist? In order to show that mammoths do not exist requires a massive effort. The entire world has been scrupulously surveyed for a moderately long period of time in order to determine if any mammoths might exist in some remote area. No evidence of any living mammoths have been found. The conclusion has been made that mammoths no longer exist. The last living mammoth died thousands of years ago. None are alive today.

Can this conclusion be reversed? Of course it can. One compelling fact - a live mammoth - would be sufficient. But until someone produces the compelling fact, the conclusion remains valid. Mammoths do not exist.

At what point does it become reasonable to assume something does not exist. In the case of the dinosaur, the evidence that the dinosaurs are totally extinct is overwhelming. Nothing has been found in the rocks of the earth to indicate that any dinosaurs existed for the last 65 million years. Furthermore, there has no authenticated sightings of these creatures in recorded history.

In order to believe in living dinosaurs some compelling evidence, such as a live dinosaur, must be forthcoming. Until such evidence is presented, dinosaurs will remain on the list of extinct creatures.

If the existence of god is given the same sort of treatment, the results are definitive. During the last few decades, the information available to humankind has increased by prodigious amounts. Our ability to send satellites into outer space has increased our knowledge about the solar system and the universe by several orders of magnitude. We now have a hundred or a thousand times as much information as was available about fifty years ago. The same sort of expansion of knowledge has been occurring in many other scientific fronts as well.

But all this new information, as well as the old, has not produced a shred of evidence that god has ever existed. This complete lack of any definitive data on the subject of god requires a reconsideration of the entire idea. The god hypothesis is a concept that has no factual support.

The god hypothesis is in the same category as the living dinosaurs. Nothing supports either concept. But the dinosaur hypothesis has a much firmer base than the god hypothesis. We do know that dinosaurs once lived on the earth. We have found many of their bones and teeth, their eggs, and droppings, impressions of their skin in the former mud, and tracks too. Dinosaurs have been shown to be real beings.

But for god the evidence is a total blank. We have nothing that indicates he ever existed. There are no photographs, no recordings of his voice, no tracks of god, no evidence of god's intervention in anything. Nothing has been found. Nothing!

Scientific study has shown a world and universe that operates without a guiding hand. Matter and energy interact in specific ways, that humankind calls the laws of nature. But intervention by a supernatural being has never been detected.

Most things that are real can be observed, measured, or somehow be shown to really exist. Facts are the basis for concluding that something exists. Without facts to support a specific concept, the concept should be considered speculative or fanciful but certainly not real. The god hypothesis has no facts to support it.

THE CREATION-EVOLUTION CONTROVERSY

Many religious leaders are apprehensive about science. They feel that science is undermining religion, and the most strident voices are raised against the scientific theory of evolution. Fundamentalist religious leaders perceive evolution as a fatal threat to their ideas. And they may be right.

Evolution has stripped off the mantle of sanctity from much of the natural world, including the origin of man. God is no longer needed to create each and every form of life on earth. Each bird, blade of grass, or ant does not have to be viewed as the specific handiwork of god. Instead, all life is viewed as part of a continuum. All the creatures of the world are inter-related, and all of them developed from one original ancestral form of life. Such a view is considered heresy by the creationists.

The creationist movement has diligently and persistently attacked science, especially the science dealing with evolution. In the process, they have declared that most of biology, much of geology, and a moderate amount of chemistry and physics are wrong.

They do not have much to support such an attack. The basis is their firmly held belief that the bible, and every word in it, is the word of god. They believe that the bible cannot be wrong.

Nothing in it can be wrong. Apparently, they fear that if one word is shown to be false, then god is suspect. So they cannot and will not permit themselves to admit that anything that they consider to be counter to the bible can possibly be right. Hence, the vigorous attack on modern science.

They insist, from blind faith, that their ideas must be right and a good portion of science must be wrong. No massive amount of evidence shakes their single-minded approach. They doggedly cling to their mis-guided idea that their fundamentalist interpretation of the bible must be correct. No series of convincing or extensive facts makes the slightest impression. Their "thinking" is like granite, it resists all attempts at penetration.

The scientific facts run counter to the creationist's ideas on a massive scale. There is no way to reconcile these differences. Obviously, one of the two views must be miserably wrong. There are a degrees of being wrong, and the two opposing positions are so far apart that one of the two has to be dismally wrong, not just wrong.

Among the absurd claims of the creationists is the age of the earth. To them, the world is young, about 6,000 to 10,000 years of age. They refuse to believe the overwhelming mass of physical evidence that decisively show that the earth is very ancient.

Creationists can look into the Grand Canyon of Arizona and claim that all the layered sedimentary rocks were deposited in the great flood of the bible.

About one mile of layered rocks are open to view in the Grand Canyon. These sedimentary rocks often contain marine fossils, showing that they must have been deposited in the ocean. A few layers were deposited on land, but most come from a marine environment.

In any undisturbed sequence of rocks, the oldest rocks must be on the bottom, and the youngest rocks on the top of the sequence. The layered rocks near the bottom of the Grand Canyon sequence contain only fossils of primitive life forms. Examination of the layers show that as the sequence moves upward, the fossil life forms continue to become more sophisticated. The rocks near the very top of the sequence contains fossils of the more sophisticated life forms. The entire sequence indicates a slow methodical deposition over extremely long periods of time. It also indicates that marine life was slowly changing and becoming more sophisticated.

The deposition of the rocks took many millions of years. Then the rocks, the entire land mass of the area, had to be raised about two miles above sea level - where they are now. And during that process, the canyon had to be cut by the Colorado river. A ponderous amount of time was necessary to wear through the rocks and carry the debris to the sea. The creationist estimate of 6,000 to 10,000 years is woefully inadequate to explain the formation of the Grand Canyon.

The Grand Canyon is not an isolated geological situation. Many other rock formations around the world present similar time requirements. The tops of the Himalayan Mountains are about 5 miles above sea level, and the rocks at the top of these mountains are composed of sedimentary layers that contain marine deposits - deposits that were formed in the ocean.

For a huge land mass like the Himalayan Mountains to move 5 miles upward in elevation is a colossal development. If we assume that normal geological processes were operating for very long periods of time, then the situation can be easily explained. But the creationists insist that it must have taken place within a ten thousand year period. To accomplish such a massive movement in such a short time span would require earth movements of gigantic magnitude, unlike anything that has been known to occur. There is no evidence of any such massive movements anywhere in the rocks of the earth.

Our known devastating earthquakes, that occasionally occur, would be trivial when compared to the events that would raise the Himalayan Mountains within a ten thousand year period. The creationist requirement that all these complex geological happenings occurred within a mere ten thousand years is totally incompatible with known geological information.

There are many more geologic features on the earth that decisively show that vast periods of time are needed in order to produce them. Mountains and valleys are mute testimony to the long periods of time needed for their formation.

The age of the earth is well known. There is little doubt in the scientific community that the age of the earth is about 4.5 to 4.6 billion years. All the scientific evidence strongly indicates that the earth is a very ancient object.

Scientists have developed a variety of methods for dating the earth. Included among these methods are: radioisotope dating, sedimentary rock deposition (exemplified by the Grand Canyon sequence), the evolution of life on earth, and astronomical information, including meteorites.

The age of the universe is known less exactly. But scientists are in general agreement that the age of the universe is between 10 and 20 billion years. An average figure of 15 billion years is often used as the age of the universe. This conclusion is based on a variety of measurements that include information about the recession of galaxies, the composition of star clusters, as well as the ratio of long half-life radioisotopes. A more exact age for the universe is under vigorous investigation right now.

But the ages of the earth and the universe are not the only problems that separate the scientific community and the creationists. Creationists believe that the present physical form of the earth is mainly due to catastrophes. They believe that the biblical flood was the source of many of these geological features. They also believe that all living things, especially humans, were created miraculously, in essentially their present form.

Most of these ideas are derived from biblical accounts, with special emphasis on the first two chapters of genesis. They devoutly quote passages from the bible that discuss the creation of the earth and the universe. They blithely ignore the fact that the bible gives two accounts of the creation - two accounts that do not agree. The logic, if the term logic can be used here, is ludicrous.

Scientific information disagrees markedly from the biblical versions. The present physical form of the earth could not have been caused mostly by catastrophes. The slow, deliberate actions of erosion, deposition, etc. have been the major cause of most of the earth's features. Certainly volcanic eruptions, and faulting have also played an important role, as well as extra-terrestrial impacts. But the major features are still due to the slow deliberate processes that are occurring every day.

The idea of a world-wide flood, as described in the bible, has no basis in fact. Our tallest mountains are about 5 miles high. In order to cover them with water, a truly vast quantity of water would be needed. Today's oceans are, about 2 miles deep. Much more additional water would be needed to raise the sea levels to cover these high mountains, than all the water known to exist on earth. Where did all this water come from? Where did all this water go after the flood was over? Nobody knows!

Furthermore, there is no evidence that the world was ever completely inundated by water. If it had happened, then most of the forms of terrestrial life would have perished. Not only would the animals have drowned, but so would most of the plants. Birds would have no where to land. Insects would be totally lost in a world that was only ocean water. And the trees, bushes, weeds, and grasses could not survive being submerged under a couple of miles of water for weeks or months. The devastation would have been a profound extinction event in the geologic record. Only aquatic life would have made it. Such a disaster did not occur.

I am aware that Noah and his ark were supposed to have saved all the creatures of the world, but such a fantastic story is extremely difficult to swallow. No single boat, or an entire flotilla of boats, could accommodate all the land forms of life on the earth. There are so many insects, spiders, lizards, snakes, rodents, herbivores, carnivores, etc. that collecting all of them would be dreadfully complicated and an immense task. Nothing even approaching such an accomplishment has ever been achieved in the most efficiently operated modern zoo, much less on one primitive boat in ancient times.

This totally ignores the plants. The plants would be needed to feed the herbivores. It might be possible to collect the seeds of all these plants and store them. But that is a gigantic cataloging task. Furthermore, the catching, collecting, and then transporting, all of these various creatures to the ark is a formidable task in logistics.

In ancient times, the new world, North and South America, were unknown. The chief means of transport was primitive by today's standards. No motor vehicles or airplanes were available. No fast communication systems were available either. The task of using the ark to save all the creatures of the world defies any reasonable explanation of how it could be done.

There are other problems with the scenario of Noah's ark. How could the snakes be prevented from eating the lizards, or the lions from devouring the antelopes, or the spiders from killing insects. How were the predators fed during this flood? How were sickness and injury handled before there was any veterinary medicine?

The biblical flood story is so full of gaping holes that there is no way to defend it. It makes no sense. Yet creationists use this story to draw conclusions about the world. Ridiculous!

There can be no doubt about it. There was no world-wide flood. The geological and biological facts do not support such an idea. Despite this scientific evidence, the creationists cling to their discredited view of the world. They refuse to accept the scientific explanation.

However, the really big problem, as far as the creationists are concerned, involves the theory of evolution - the concept originally proposed by Darwin about 135 years ago. The creationists doggedly insist that each and every specific form of life was created by a special act of the creator - a miracle.

There are over two million different species of creatures described in the scientific literature.

There are probably several additional million species that have not been described. But there are the much larger number of species found only as fossils. More than 99% of all the known species that ever existed are now extinct. According to the creationists, each and every one of these species was a special work of the creator - a miracle. All forms of life that ever lived on the earth requires a gosh-awful lot of miracles.

However, the theory of evolution has a much simpler and more logical explanation for all this diversity of life. Miracles are not required. The vast assortment of all life forms can be explained if we assume that all of these life forms had a common ancestry. Each specific life form slowly diverged from similar forms. Over the course of millions and billions of years, the changes resulted in the complex variety of life we now have on the earth.

Since Darwin first proposed the concept of evolution, the scientific community has been diligently studying the idea. About 135 years of effort have been expended and have resulted in billions of scientific facts about many forms of life. This information strongly suggests that evolution has happened.

There is an enormous amount of data on this subject. It involves fossils, comparison of modern life forms, analysis of the biochemistry of organisms, etc. This information is comprehensive and complex. I do not want to bog down in a lengthy review of all this information. Instead I will attempt to concentrate on the life about us today.

If we study various creatures living today, the minor differences are obvious as well as the strikingly similar features. For example, the lion and the tiger, the dog and the wolf, and the horse and the donkey are all similar pairs of animals. It is easy to conclude that the lion and the tiger are both cats. The lion and the tiger have similar traits, but possess features that are unique for their species. A mating between a lion and a tiger produces a hybrid, a liger, which is usually sterile.

The same sort of comparison applies to the wolf and dog. They both are obviously canines and it easy to differentiate between a wolf and a poodle. It is not so easy to differentiate between a wolf and a malamute. The wolf and the dog are closely related. They can mate and produce viable offspring.

The horse and the donkey are also related creatures. A mating between these produces a mule. Mules are usually sterile and seldom can reproduce. However, a mating between a tiger and a wolf would not produce any offspring. Neither will a mating between a horse and a dog. They are too distantly related for that.

These relatively simple observations have now been reinforced by studies involving biochemistry. The biochemistry of various species is unique for each species. However, for species that have similar macro features, the biochemistry is very similar. The biochemistry of the lion and tiger would be very similar. While the biochemistry of the tiger and the wolf would be less similar. The biochemistry of a tiger and a horse would be even less similar.

To carry this a bit further, the biochemistry of a horse and a donkey would be very similar. The same sort of similarity would occur between the biochemistry of a dog and a wolf. However, the biochemistry of a dog and a donkey would be considerably less similar.

The generalizations that result form this type of study are significant. The more similar the macro-features of an organism, the more similar their biochemistry is. There are a few situations where survival requirements impinge on this idea. For example, a dolphin and a shark are both similarly streamlined for movement through the water. Yet they are markedly distinct in many other ways. Dolphins breathe air using their lungs, while sharks get their oxygen from water using their gills. Despite their similar streamlined structure, many of their physical features are noticeably different. The shark and the dolphin are not closely related despite their similar outward appearance.

All of the millions of life forms on the earth are composed of the same type of material. The biochemistry of widely divergent forms have much in common. The reason is that all of the life forms on earth are made mostly from the same distinct molecules - about fifty molecules. Water is the common solvent in all life forms. There are twenty amino acids used for making all the proteins found in earthly life. Five base molecules are used for making all the DNA and RNA throughout the life system. Glucose is the molecule used to make all the various types of cellulose and starches. The limited number of biochemicals that make up most of the life system is astounding.

The similar building blocks of life make it possible for human beings to eat a wide assortment of foods. Chicken, fish, beef, pork, walnuts, carrots, lettuce, mushrooms, apples, and grapes are all suitable foods. So are: corn, potatoes, rice, strawberries, watermelons, oranges, lobster, clams, and venison. The list goes on and on. Even exotic items like: rattlesnake and octopus are considered delicacies by some gourmets.

But the important truth, demonstrated by our diverse eating habits, is that all of the multitude of foods are made, more or less, from the same stuff. Despite the obvious differences in external appearances, the major building blocks - the molecules of the life process - are mostly the same in all the assorted creatures we eat as food. Our eating behaviors strongly suggests that all forms of life are related. We all have a lot in common.

The scientific study of the biochemistry of living systems reinforces this idea most emphatically. Practically all of the life forms on earth are made mostly from the same fifty molecules. This is an astounding fact! Even though many millions of molecules are known, only about fifty molecules comprise most of what we call life.

Creationist are especially antagonistic about comparisons between man and the chimpanzee. Scientists consider the chimpanzee a close relative. The pygmy chimpanzee, renamed the bonobo, is the closest relative to humankind. Bonobos are limited in number in the wild and have not been as thoroughly studied as the common chimpanzee. I will discuss the relationship of human beings and the common chimpanzee because we have so much more available information.

Some amazing similarities are found when we compare the chimpanzee to man. A cursory examination shows that the chimpanzee bears a striking resemblance to man. Careful scrutiny of chimpanzee behavior shows some remarkable similarities to human behavior. However, the comparison of the biochemistry of the common chimpanzee and man is the most definitive comparison.

The chimpanzee's biochemistry is about 98% to 99% identical to man's. That is not only the fundamental building blocks of life, but also in the sequence in which these units are assembled within the living system.

The beta chain of hemoglobin has been studied extensively and included the comparison of the chimpanzee and man, as well as the gorilla and man. The beta chain of hemoglobin contains 146 amino acids in an orderly sequence. There are only twenty amino acids that are used to make the beta chain of hemoglobin. Each individual amino acid is added to the chain in a specific sequence.

Mathematically, there is an astronomically huge number of possible arrangements.

When a comparison of the sequence of amino acids in the beta chain of hemoglobin was made between the human and the gorilla, only one difference was found. One amino acid out of the 146 amino acids in the sequence was different. The biochemistry of the gorilla and man are very similar.

However, when the comparison was made between the sequence of amino acids in the beta chain of hemoglobin for the common chimpanzee and man, the two sequences were identical. This indicates that man and chimpanzee are very closely related. Even though man is related to the gorilla, the relationship to the chimpanzee is closer.

Studies of other common biochemicals show similar striking resemblances between the chimpanzee and man. Such studies are continuing. At this point, the biochemical information is continuing to indicate that the chimpanzee and man are closely related. This similarity between the chimpanzee and man makes many religious people uncomfortable. That is not what they want to believe.

If we carry the chimpanzee and man comparison a step further, into the religious realm, a dilemma is presented. Modern day religions usually classify the chimpanzee as an animal, without an immortal soul. Human beings, from the religious viewpoint, possess an immortal soul.

Scientific evidence from anthropology indicates that human beings slowly and gradually developed from more primitive forms. During the last few million years a variety of species were involved. Some of these included the following: Homo habilis, Homo erectus, Neandertal man, archaic Homo sapiens, etc. Just when, in the evolution of man from the more primitive state, did the immortal soul appear. Was Neandertal man a true human with an immortal soul? Was Homo erectus? How can anyone decide? And if they do decide, how can they determine if their decision is correct?

But there is a more vexing aspect to this awkward situation. Man and the chimpanzee are so closely related that a mating between the two would very likely produce an offspring. Would this resulting hybrid of half man and half chimpanzee have an immortal soul, or would it be relegated into the class of a typical animal without an immortal soul? If a decision is made either way, how can one determine if it is correct?

We can carry this a step further. Suppose the half man - half chimpanzee were mated with another human. The offspring would now be about 3/4ths human from a genetic point of view. Does this offspring have an immortal soul? Suppose the matings were continued, with resulting offspring being about 87% human, then about 94% human and then about 97%. When, if ever, does the offspring from these matings inherit an immortal soul? But the most awkward part is, how can anyone determine this attribute?

The scientific information linking man and the chimpanzee, gorilla, gibbon, and orangutan is most disturbing to creationists. They are appalled that the scientific evidence is so thorough. They can see no way out of the situation except to try to discredit the scientific community and science in general. The creationists realize that their religious position is becoming more and more untenable as more and more information is collected by the scientific community. Nevertheless, in the face of overwhelming odds, the creationists persist.

A WRONG HYPOTHESIS

The creation-evolution controversy illustrates the damage and wasted effort that can result from a false hypothesis. The creationist devoutly and sincerely believe that they are right. They think that their cause is just and they "know" that god is on their side.

But the strangest part of all this entire situation is that the creationists have not examined the validity of their basic concept - god. They are assuming that the god hypothesis is correct. And that is where the problem begins. When someone "knows" that something is correct, they assume there is no need to examine the concept. That is a fundamental error.

A wrong hypothesis leads to all sorts of difficulties, whether it is in science or religion. A wrong hypothesis in science causes scientific researchers to perform pointless experiments that lead to nowhere. A wrong hypothesis does much the same thing in the religious area. Energy and effort are squandered in wrong approaches, instead of being directed into meaningful endeavors.

The creationists are trying desperately to suppress scientific information, instead of encouraging scientific effort. Creationists, like almost everyone else, want to see cancer cured, want to solve the energy problems of the world, and want to have a host of difficulties corrected. Yet their actions are having exactly the opposite effect. Progress in education and science in particular has been noticeably slowed by their persistent efforts at suppression of valid scientific information, especially about evolution.

The creation movement has been quietly successful for many years. The concept of evolution and the name of Charles Darwin had been essentially eliminated from the textbooks used in the junior high schools and senior high schools of this country. Creationists do not hesitate to pressure and coerce teachers who attempt to teach evolution in the schools. Some state legislatures have passed laws requiring equal time in the classrooms for the creationists preposterous ideas. The creationists ideas about the origin of species and the age of the earth have been shown to be miserably wrong by the scientific community. Yet they want such wrong information taught as science in the schools.

Creationists have been guilty of deliberately and diligently suppressing valid scientific information on a large scale. They are still trying to do so. Their efforts have added to the intellectual impoverishment of our children concerning valid scientific ideas. Our youth have incomplete and distorted ideas about the world and the universe because of this suppression of information. The scientific illiteracy of the American public is partially due to the sustained efforts of creationists and their supporters.

We should no longer tolerate such blatant abuse of information in the name of religion. Such thought control is obnoxious. Wrong is wrong no matter what guise it may assume. Wrapping wrong ideas under the mantle of a deity does not make them right.

Anyone with an open mind and some fundamental ideas about rational thought processes will quickly realize that the creationists ideas are sterile of any constructive or useful concepts. Furthermore, their ideas are often directly opposed to scientific theories. The creationists are anti-science in the extreme.

The creationists have declared war on science, and they vocally insist that their ideas be adopted and taught in the schools. Creationists have stirred up the animosity of many patient scientists, who have assumed that everyone would recognize what is correct and what is false. Many scientists are realizing that the attempts to replace valid scientific information with religious dogma must be stopped. The creationists "know" that their interpretation of the bible must be right. They will not consider anything else.

The fundamental problem lies in the belief system. The basic premise could be false. The fundamental hypothesis of the creationists may be wrong. They think there is a god, and there probably isn't. Almost everything that springs forth from a wrong hypothesis may be fatally flawed.

KNOWABLE UNIVERSE

The very idea of a super being in total control of the universe is most disturbing. Supposedly, this god can change anything, at any time, if he so desires. That would mean that the universe would be unknowable. Because of the arbitrary intervention of this god, the universe would be fundamentally unstable. The capricious or whimsical behavior of this god would be superimposed on the orderly behavior of the laws of nature.

Events would not have to follow a predictable cause and effect relationship. Almost anything could happen, at any moment, for no apparent reason. Scientists would be confronted with phenomena that defied a logical deduction. The actions of a god would create confusion and disarray in science.

This unwanted, unexpected, and illogical intervention by any super being has never been observed. Despite all the vast accumulation of events and phenomena that have been studied by scientific personnel, no sudden, capricious, or unexplainable event or phenomena have ever been observed. Scientific study gives every indication that the universe is completely orderly. Events and phenomena invariably follow the laws of nature.

Scientific study has shown that the universe is knowable. By that I mean that it is possible to understand how the universe formed and to understand what is happening now. We have determined that the natural laws are obeyed by the particles and objects that make up the universe.

Gravity is an outstanding example of what I am referring to. Our space engineers and astronomers have been able to calculate the various gravimetric tugs that a space vehicle would receive from various objects in space. That includes: the sun, moon, planets, asteroids, etc. By means of these calculations, we have been able to send space probes into the far reaches of our solar system.

Even though planets like Uranus and Neptune are over a billion miles away, our space probes have rendezvoused with them within a few miles of the values calculated here on earth. In the process, the gravitational effects of the huge planets, like Jupiter and Saturn, had to be incorporated into the calculations as well as the perturbations caused by smaller bodies like Mars.

To make a very long story short, our scientists know how gravity works and they know that the bodies of the solar system obey the law of gravity. That is what makes such long and complicated space flights possible. Natural laws are obeyed.

If and unseen hand, like the hand of god, should suddenly intervene and change something in a capricious or arbitrary manner, then such a successful flight would not be possible.

I have used space flight for a demonstration of the way the particles and objects in the universe obey natural laws. Similar analogies could be made with charged particles. Plus charged particles repel each other. Oppositely charged particles attract each other. Magnetic lines of force influence the path of moving charge particles. All of these effects obey the laws of nature. The behavior is often expressed in mathematical equations. The adherence to natural laws is exact.

Once again, if the influence of an unseen hand, a god, interfered in any of these behaviors, the laws of nature would be violated. Things would not always behave in an exact mathematical way. There would be arbitrary variations depending on the whims of the god. Equations would not be able to express these whimsical differences. The universe would be unknowable.

The events and phenomena that occur in our world and in our universe obey a cause and effect relationship. Humankind has come a long way toward understanding how both the world and the universe operate. There is every reason to expect additional understanding will result from further studies. Such a universe is patently more comfortable than one that relies on a god. Such a universe would be one in which anything and everything can, and does, get modified by the deity.

But scientists have never detected such arbitrary switches in behavior. Everything remains exact. The charge on an electron is always minus one. The charge on a proton is always plus one. These charges are equal and opposite. The values do not oscillate. The charges remain fixed.

That makes the universe knowable. If a god was tinkering endlessly with nature, then the universe would not be knowable. Apparently god does not exercise any influence on the universe.

SCIENTIFIC ANALYSIS OF THE GOD HYPOTHESIS

Let's examine the scientific method in more detail, especially the way it might be applied to religious ideas.

When a scientist is presented with an hypothesis, there is a procedure to follow that will indicate whether the hypothesis is reasonable or not. First and foremost the question can be asked, "Does the hypothesis conform to all the known facts?"

An example of a hypothesis might be that, "silicon dioxide (sand) can be converted into water." A scientist would seriously question this hypothesis because the mass of a silicon dioxide unit is more than three times the mass of water. If such a transformation occurred, then the scientific law, the conservation of mass, would be wrong. And the law of conservation of mass has been tested so many times that it is now a firmly established generalization in science. So the hypothesis of sand into water is in serious trouble from the very beginning.

The next step would involve a search through the scientific literature to see if any previous work had shown such a transformation might occur. No scientist in the past found anything pertinent on the subject.

Despite the poor beginnings of this hypothesis study, a scientist might still decide to do some experimentation in an attempt to determine if silicon dioxide can be changed into water. He could place silicon dioxide in a high temperature furnace and determine if any water was formed. Or he could place it in a high pressure device to see if any water formed. Or he could bombard silicon dioxide with high energy radiation to see if any water formed. A variety of experiments might be devised.

After a somewhat lengthy study, in which no water was formed, the scientist might conclude that the law of conservation of mass must still be true and that silicon dioxide does not transform into water. He would conclude that the hypothesis is false.

The god hypothesis should receive the same sort of treatment. The god hypothesis states that a supreme being created and now controls the entire universe. However, the hypothesis runs into trouble almost immediately. The law of conservation of mass applies here as well.

How did this supreme being create the universe from nothing? The idea violates the fundamental law of conservation of mass. But this poses an even bigger question. Where did the creator come from? What is the origin of this all-powerful being? By invoking god, we are simply moving the origin of the universe back to the supreme being. But now we have failed to explain the origin of the supreme being. All the concept of a supreme being does is cloud up the situation. It certainly does not help to explain anything.

Even though the starting hypothesis is filled with uncertainties, a scientist might not stop the study because of this. He could consult the scientific literature and see what other scientists have developed about this hypothesis. He would discover, if he did not know it already, that there is a plausible scientific explanation for the origin of the universe. It is called the Big Bang theory.

The Big Bang theory is an idea that has withstood the test of time. It was originally proposed about 70 years ago, and has been studied diligently ever since. The Big Bang theory is a firmly established generalization that conforms to all the known facts about our universe. No magic or supernatural events are needed in this explanation. The laws of nature are all obeyed.

Furthermore, the Big Bang theory has predicted a variety of phenomena that have been found. The biggest triumph of this theory is the cosmic background radiation that permeates the entire universe. The Big Bang theory predicted that this radiation would be everywhere in the universe and permitted the calculation of the wavelengths that would be found. It explained phenomena that, at the time, were not even known.

The Big Bang theory satisfactorily explains all the known facts we have about our universe. And we have amassed a prodigious quantity of information.

But the god hypothesis is of no help in explaining anything. The statement, "God did it." is of no help in predicting anything. However, if god did do it, then there must be some mechanism for bringing this about. How is this control exercised? Nobody knows.

Scientists have been interested in forces, and have studied them extensively. So far, four forces have been discovered. Gravity is one, coulombic attraction is another, and there are forces within the nucleus of atoms, called the strong nuclear force and the weak nuclear force. Scientists are currently engaged in attempts to combine these four forces into an overall principle.

The situation regarding forces is very clear. The four known forces can explain everything that we encounter in our world and our universe. Unfortunately, a god force has never been detected, despite the myriad of instruments and sensing devices that have been used and are still being used. Not one scientific fact supports the idea of a god force.

There is a fundamental rule of physics that states, "A body in motion will remain in motion until acted upon by a force. A body at rest will remain at rest, until acted upon by a force." The universe is made up of matter and energy, and interactions between matter and energy have been thoroughly studied. During all these studies, no evidence of a supernatural force has ever been detected.

The only conceivable way that god can control the universe is to exert some force upon the matter within it. But there is not a single documented instance of such an event.

Doors do not open unless someone or something exerts a force against the door. Doors can be blown open or closed by the wind, by the push of a cat, or a dog, or a human being. But doors do not swing open or closed unless acted upon by a force. An energy source is needed before a door can be moved.

In some extreme cases, it could be due to the quiver of the earth as an earthquake takes place, or the settling of the house when the foundation shifts. But logical and natural forces account for all door openings. No magic is involved.

A scientist searching through the scientific literature would find nothing to support the god hypothesis. Nevertheless, the scientist could then try experimentation.

He could set a pendulum swinging and pray to god so that the oscillations would change in an unexpected way. He could raise two sets of plants. One set would get regular tap water, the other set of plants would get regular tap water that had been blessed. Would the effect of the blessing have any effect on the plants that were grown?

He could also study statistics with respect to accidents. Some people think that a St. Christopher medal provides protection from accidents. Other people get their boats blessed as a protection from accidents. A comparison of matched groups might show the influence of a supernatural power.

A multitude of such experiments might be devised and tried. It would be a means of actually determining the validity of the god hypothesis. I am unwilling to perform these experiments myself. I would expect all of these to be indecisive or inconclusive. But someone, with more motivation than I, should perform such experiments. Try to discover if there is any validity to the god hypothesis.

But now let us suppose that someone did perform hundreds of such experiments and found nothing to support the god hypothesis. (That is what I would expect.) At this point, the persons performing all these tests, and everyone else too, should conclude that there is nothing to support the god hypothesis.

A hypothesis unsupported by scientific facts has no merit. It becomes pointless to pursue it further. In order to continue to consider an hypothesis seriously, it must be supported by facts, collected by experimentation and observation. Otherwise the hypothesis must join the long list of sterile hypotheses, such as the transformation of silicon dioxide into water. Furthermore, a scientist should not use an ill founded hypothesis as the basis of additional work.

That is the status of the god hypothesis. It is totally sterile. There is not a single shred of evidence that god exists.

When we consider that the god hypothesis has been studied, to some extent, for about 200 years using scientific procedures and nothing decisive has been found, it warrants a conclusion. The god hypothesis has nothing substantial to support it. The god hypothesis should be set aside, until something definite can be established about it. At the moment it falls into the category of wishful thinking - nothing more.

GUIDING PRINCIPLES OF SCIENCE

Although the vast majority of the human population of the world believe in god, the concept has not been tested for its possible validity. The god concept is of great importance to many people and often influences almost everything they do. The god concept is firmly rooted in the traditions of humankind. Uprooting such a well established idea would require a mammoth effort. Nevertheless, there is enough information available to draw a plausible conclusion about the god concept.

The big question is, "Is there any logical way to determine if god really exists?" The answer is, that a very reasonable conclusion is now possible concerning this important idea. That is what the book is about.

The question about the reality of god has remained intractable since the beginning of civilization. The question was intractable about 1000 years ago, and perhaps even 100 years ago. But today the question can be answered.

The reason for the change is the vast amount of information that is now available. Much of this information was not available even a few short years ago. Procedures have been developed that are routinely used on difficult problems. The term, the scientific method, is used to characterize these procedures.

The scientific method is fundamental logic applied to a specific situation. The scientific method is a relatively simple procedure, that does produce results.

In science there are a series of general statements that are the basis for much of our understanding of matter, energy, the world, and the universe. The mass of information and measurements collected by scientific investigators forms the basis for making these generalizations. The generalizations fall into three categories: hypotheses, laws, and theories.

An hypothesis is a preliminary guess on how phenomena might be explained. First the hypothesis is stated. Then the hypothesis is examined in detail. The scientific method can be used to ascertain whether an hypothesis is correct. Various operations, experiments, observations, measurements, etc. are made in order to determine if the hypothesis is true or false.

Very often, in science, there are competing hypothesis on a given subject. The scientific method provides a means of determining which of the competing hypotheses is more suitable for explaining the phenomena under investigation.

Information is collected on various aspects of the competing ideas. As the study unfolds each hypothesis is examined to determine how well it may conform to the facts that have been collected. Eventually, the facts tend to support one hypothesis over the other and in a real lopsided contest, one hypothesis is soundly rejected as unsuitable to explain the phenomena.

An hypothesis is a mere beginning in the generalizations. Laws usually are considerably narrower in scope than theories.

One of the familiar natural laws is the law of gravity. Stated simply, it means that on earth, things fall down, toward the center of the earth, not up. If a person steps off the roof of a building, that person will plunge to the ground. This happens every time. There are no known deviations. If someone disregards a natural law, it can result in disaster.

Scientific theories are broad generalizations that encompass a wide series of phenomena. Theories are the backbone of science. Theories do not have to be rigidly correct in every tiny detail. However, the guiding ideas must have wide application.

Some examples of theories are: the Big Bang theory, the atomic theory, the theory of evolution, etc. Each of these theories encompasses a broad area of science. The Big Bang not only explains the formation of the universe, but also helps explain a wide assortment of astronomical information.

The atomic theory summarizes the massive data collected about atomic particles, and provides the basis for understanding the composition and organization of our world and our universe. The theory of evolution provides a comprehensive explanation for the myriad forms of life on earth. It provides an understanding for a bewildering array of biological information.

Scientific laws are such firmly established generalizations that they seldom are modified. However, theories are more flexible. There is a continual reappraisal and reevaluation of the status of scientific theories with respect to the facts that have accumulated. Occasional modifications in existing theories are made. That is how science progresses. The concepts that form the basis for science are gradually reworked to provide a clearer. more meaningful explanation for phenomena. In a sense, all the theories of science are tentative. Nevertheless, scientific theories represent the very best explanations, that humankind has devised, for natural phenomena.

But do not be misled. Despite the tentative nature of science, the accomplishments are truly impressive. Science has been, and still is, most successful. Flights has been made into outer space, and distant planets have been photographed and visited by our vehicles. Hydrogen bombs have been detonated. Nuclear reactors propel naval vessels. Potent drugs have been made to alleviate and eradicate certain illnesses. Synthetic fibers are used to make clothing and rugs. Mineral and petroleum deposits have been located all over the globe.

Science has been eminently successful. It has given us so many things we want and need. Warm homes in winter, cool homes in summer. We can listen to the radio, or watch television, or go to a theater and see a movie. Automobiles and airplanes take us to where we want to go. The list of scientific accomplishments goes on and on.

Unfortunately, some religious leaders bemoan science. Yet these same individuals do not hesitate to partake of the accomplishments of science. They wear clothing made of synthetic fibers, receive antibiotics and other medicines when they are ill, use the telephone and electric lights, and drive their cars as needed.

Despite this participation in the fruits of science, they criticize science as the cause of much of the world's ills. They claim that science is basically wrong in much of its undertakings. They vehemently resist many of the basic claims of science, such as the age of the earth or the age of the universe. How can anything so spectacularly successful as science be so wrong? Science is essentially correct. Some of these religious leaders are just plain wrong.

INTELLIGENT LIFE ELSEWHERE

A little speculation is in order. There are about 50 billion galaxies in the universe. Our Milky Way galaxy is but one of these enormous number of galaxies.

The milky Way galaxy is composed of about 500 billion stars. And our sun is but one of the 500 billion stars. We know that intelligent life does exist in our solar system - on planet earth. So far we have not been able to detect intelligent life anywhere else in our galaxy. The search is continuing.

But let's speculate about the 50 billion galaxies. If there is one intelligent life form in our galaxy, there probably is intelligent life in other galaxies as well. If we assume that there is only one intelligent life form in each galaxy then there could be 50 billion intelligent life systems in the universe. That is an awful lot of intelligent life.

Even if we want to be conservative and assume that only one out of every fifty galaxies has an intelligent life, there would be a billion intelligent societies out there. That is still an enormous number of intelligent worlds.

If we think god had a ponderous chore keeping track of the world and all its people, try to imagine how impossible a task of a billion intelligent worlds would be.

I know intelligent life is speculation. But it is reasonable speculation. What are the 50 billion galaxies doing out there anyway? They are made out of the same stuff as the Milky Way galaxy. They have stars, gas clouds, and super novas, much like our galaxy does. Conditions must be somewhat similar in some of these galaxies. It would not be surprising if intelligent life did exist in some of these galaxies, We should expect it to be there.

The problem with finding life in another galaxy is the enormous distances between them and us. The Andromeda nebula is the closest big galaxy to our Milky Way and is about 2 million light years away. If they could somehow send a signal that we could receive today, the problem of a communication lag appears.

If the earth prepared and sent a response next year, it would take about 2 million years for the signal to reach the Andromeda nebula. If they did receive it and replied quickly, then in another 2 million years we would receive their response. Imagine! It would take about 4 million years before we knew, that they knew, that we knew. That is a most severe communication problem. And remember that time lag is for the closest big galaxy. All the other big galaxies would take much longer.

What I am driving at with all this. I simply believe that the 50 billion galaxies are not just wandering around the universe. I think things are happening there that are much like what is happening here. And I find it most difficult to imagine any one super being - any god - managing the entire universe. It is a colossally impossible task.

Some very recent work with a Mars meteorite reinforces the idea that life may exist in other worlds. The information discovered in the analysis of the Mars meteorite is suggestive but not compelling. Almost everyone would like to know that life did exist on Mars at some time in the past. But we must not let our enthusiasm carry us too far.

The evidence found is extremely interesting. It reinforces the idea that essential organic molecules do form spontaneously under primitive conditions on planets. This is the first time that organic molecules have been shown to be on Mars. The Mars meteorite data tends to reinforce the ideas about the origin of life on the earth.

If life did form in the early history of Mars, then it would mean that life can easily form on a planet that has liquid water. The probabilities that life exists elsewhere would be increased tremendously. If life does form so easily, we should expect to find life throughout our Milky Way galaxy. And the more life that forms, the higher the chances that intelligent life will appear.

Life on Mars would change our entire view of intelligent life in the universe. We would expect intelligent life to be much more common than we do now. If that were the case, there may be thousands, even millions of intelligent societies in our Milky Way galaxy. There could be thousands or even millions of intelligent societies in all 50 billion galaxies in the universe. The total number of intelligent worlds could soar into the trillions or beyond.

But before we get too carried away, we must restrain our excitement and recognize that additional data is needed before we can say anything definitive about life on Mars. Perhaps there was life on Mars. Perhaps there was not. No one can say for sure.

Chapter 4

POSSIBLE EFFECTS OF WRITING THIS BOOK

SCIENTIFIC PERSONNEL

Scientific personnel are caught in a dilemma. They have been taught from birth that god and religion are good. That being a church-going believer in god is the way to be. Any scientist is much like any other human being, he or she wants to have the cozy security afforded by the supreme being in the sky.

But in order to become a working scientist, the individual went to some school, college, or university and learned how to think independently. He or she was asked to examine various concepts and decide their appropriateness for given situations. Future scientists are trained to think. As scientists they were also trained to be skeptical of various ideas and to try to determine which of various competing ideas might be the most appropriate.

As scientists they learned about the laws of nature and how these laws were discovered. They learned that these natural laws were reliable. They also learned about different types of phenomena encountered in the real world, including: energy, radiation, atoms, molecules, nuclear particles, etc. They learned that all matter and energy conform to these natural laws.

In a way. they were being presented with two different sets of instructions. One set came from loving parents and the other came from skilled, knowledgeable teachers. There was a basic disagreement in the two sets of instructions. Most scientists ignore the clash. They, more or less, refuse to think seriously about it. An individual scientist often does not know what to do about the clash of ideas and ends up doing nothing.

But any knowledgeable scientist should do something. When something is broke, you fix it. Each scientist knows that the fundamental tenants of science are correct. He or she has often done a certain amount of scientific investigation work that gives him or her a first hand knowledge of the basic ideas of science. Nevertheless, the individual scientist has been indoctrinated about god from the cradle on. And what is foremost, the individual scientist wants to believe in god. The god concept seems to fill a basic human need. It is somewhat irresistible.

However, any thinking scientist must be able to recognize that most of the statements about god by religious people have no basis in fact. They should know that the idea of a super being running the entire universe is somewhat out of step with reality.

Each scientist should really try to examine the idea of god from a totally dispassionate point of view. That won't be easy for many. Treat the god hypothesis as though it were a science project. Is this idea correct? What evidence is there for this idea? Why should I believe such an idea?

But no scientist, worthy of the name, should criticize anyone who does not believe in god, before he or she examines the facts. First and foremost, some firm evidence that there is a god must be found. As any scientist knows, scientific facts are compelling.

But if any scientist follows this procedure, he or she will end up just about where I am now. Not one solid scientific fact can be found that shows the existence of god. There is nothing!

It is amazing. Despite the many millions of scientific measurements, observations, calculations, etc. not a single fact demonstrates that god exists. That failure to find anything should be very compelling. Any scientist should not ignore facts, nor the lack of facts.

SCIENTIST'S THINKING

The typical scientist of today knows that science has been very successful. However, he or she knows that it would be nice to be able to retain the age old security blanket of religion. It would be nice if it could work both ways.

Here is religion on one hand saying that god controls everything, and science which clearly demonstrates that god controls nothing. The individual scientist must know, deep down, that such a dichotomy should not go on. Either the rational, sensible view of science prevails, or the irrational religious view dominates. Trying to juggle the two concepts in some sort of compromise is not a satisfactory solution.

The path from being a believer in god, to a doubter of god, to the certain knowledge that the whole concept is a fraud, takes time - a lot of time. Such a transformation in thinking will not happen overnight. But with a lot of agonizing and introspection it can be done.

The scientist of today must confront reality and discard irrationality. Science is strictly rational. No mumbo-jumbo explanations. Science is based on facts and without facts there is little to go on.

Logical, rational thinking shows, very clearly, that religious ideas are based on fantasy. They make a series of claims and hopes that can not be delivered. Their only reality is in the minds of human beings. And it is in the mind that rational thoughts must occur. Cluttering up the thought process of the mind with fiction, emotional fiction, is a severe impediment to a rational thought process. Religious nonsense has got to go.

Do not be alarmed by discarding religion. Once the transition is made from believer to non-believer, there is no drastic change in behavior. Morality does not disappear. Neither does honesty, concern for your fellow humans, or any altruism you might have had. The overall view of the world situation becomes much clearer and finely focused than before. Everything stands out unencumbered by the god concept. No longer is everything filtered through a supernatural state. Things are dealt with directly.

When something is done, it has a logical reason, not a make believe one. The web of irrational thinking tends to be dispersed. You become free of fantasy. You can think clearly.

THE SCIENTIFIC COMMUNITY

The present attitude of the scientific community is doing a disservice to humankind. Scientific spokesman, for various scientific organizations, usually make bland statements about science and religion. They have said that science and religion are completely separate activities and have nothing in common. Furthermore, they often add that science has nothing to say about religion.

Such behavior is a complete dodging of the issue. I think that scientists have a great deal to say about religion, if they had the intestinal fortitude to do so. Even the statement, that science has nothing to say about religion, actually speaks volumes.

Science deals with the real world - all aspects of it. Science deals with matter, energy, and the interactions between matter and energy. Scientific study involves almost every conceivable facet of the world and the universe. Various established disciplines include: mathematics, biology, geology, chemistry, physics, astronomy, etc. Everything that is part of the real world, the real universe, has been under the probing scrutiny of science.

And after all this study, scientific spokesmen say that science has nothing to say about religion. Scientific spokesmen also say that science and religion are separate and independent endeavors. What can these statements mean? How is it that science has nothing to say about religion?

The answer is simple. Science deals with the real world - reality. Religion must deal with the world of make believe. Religion is outside the scope of science. Fantasy has no place in science. That is why science and religion are separate endeavors. That is why science has nothing to say about religion.

Each and every scientist, who considers himself or herself a religious person, should reexamine their position. The world needs clear, rational thinking by everyone, especially scientific personnel. The cobwebs of irrational thinking go along with many religious concepts. The religious ideas often have very little to do with reality. They confuse and obscure a clear rational view.

Discuss the issue with your scientific associates. It might be advisable to perform experiments to test the validity of the god hypothesis. Make use of the scientific method. But do something! Ignoring the problem of science and religion will not make it go away.

THE RELIGIOUS COMMUNITY'S RESPONSE

The fate of anyone who seriously questions the beliefs of any religious group is not good. Religious groups are very good at fending off attacks. They have devised an extensive vocabulary for use in such circumstances.

Two of the favorite words are agnostic and atheist. Atheist is especially effective. To the faithful, atheist denotes total insensitivity. It is a complete shutoff of the mind from the concept of god. An atheist is a poor, misguided, unthinking wretch who dismisses the whole religion business with scorn and ridicule.

On the other hand, few religious people consider themselves to be theists - one who believes in god. This term is seldom used to designate a believer. But atheist is quickly used to pinpoint a non-believer.

The term godless is also used regularly. This seems to denote a complete lack of morality or ethics. The idea seems to be that if one believes in god, that person behaves honorably and performs good deeds. But a godless person must be immoral, unethical, and in general despicable.

Actually, these ideas are way off the mark. People who have thought about the god situation are thinking people. A so-called atheist has spent a lot of time pondering the whole scenario. Reaching the conclusion that god does not exist is not a happy conclusion. It may be a realistic one, but it does not convey a sense of joy.

Realizing that there is no god does not change the morality of a non-believer. A non-believer makes their personal behavior patterns more definite. They now must depend on their own self image, not the interpretation that might be placed on their behavior by a deity. Non-believers do the right thing for the right reasons. They want to help their fellow man, they want to make life more pleasant and harmonious. They are not trying to please some remote god. Being a non-believer does not accelerate the degeneration of morality or ethics.

Down through the centuries, being a believer did not eliminate lying, cheating, stealing, etc. from the behavior of the believers. Being a believer does not make a person moral. Believers have been guilty of all kinds of crimes and atrocities.

Among the repertoire of words that descend on anyone challenging the idea of a super being are: blasphemy, sacrilege, and infidel. Blasphemy is the profane abuse of god and sacred things, or a contempt for god. Sacrilege is the desecration of what is sacred. Infidel means an unbeliever, a heathen.

These words and phrases descend on the non-believer. But a more sanctimonious way of dealing with infidels is to declare that the non-believer has become possessed by the devil. This sort of transforms the unbeliever into the devil. And that wraps it up for the faithful. What more needs to be said? The unbeliever permeates evil. He is doomed to hellfire. He becomes a menace to everyone who is good and holy.

The price for speaking out is high. An unbeliever will be shunned, ostracized, frowned upon, and become the object of fear. And all of these actions will be taken in the name of god, for holiness and virtue, for the good of the home, etc.

The punishment should fit the crime. And what is the crime? The crime is thinking and deducing plausible conclusions. The crime is not agreeing with the vast majority of the population.

Is the world ready to accept correct conclusions about god? Probably not! People do not want to lose god. The removal of god from their lives would leave them empty and exposed. The big security blanket in the sky would be torn to tatters and disappear.

The faithful do not seem to realize that there is nothing to lose. They seem to forget, or refuse to believe, that the god concept is almost certainly worthless. The believers ignore the problems generated by religions. They just condemn the perceived attacker.

That is the procedure that is followed in a courtroom, when the defendant has no case at all. Attack the district attorney and his associates. Picture them as being: unreasonable, unfair, unjust, unethical, etc. The district attorney and his associates end up being on trial. The guilt or innocence of the defendant are totally lost in the ensuing melee. Unfortunately, such diversionary tactics occasionally prove successful.

But the essence, or gist, of what I have written in this book does not really lie in my attributes as an individual. Rather, it lies in the validity of the approach and the clearness of the conclusions.

If anyone wants to refute the ideas in this book, facts are needed. Words alone will not do it. Facts, and only facts, will refute the ideas presented. Words of condemnation are just so much hot air.

It would be nice to really know there is a god, if it were actually true. But in order for me to alter my view, I need facts - firm, solid facts. Nothing else will suffice.

CLERGY'S PLIGHT

I feel sorry for any clergy who read this book. They will be placed in a most uncomfortable position. One scientist is informing them that they have been duped for their entire lives. They spent years in theology and divinity school studying about god. I know there are a lot of other things involved, but the big focus was on god. If he is not there, the entire exercise becomes a big farce.

The mantle of sanctity, in which the clergy are wrapped, should be dropped. Clergy call themselves reverend. But this phraseology should be eliminated. Clergy will once again become ordinary people. What a letdown!

The members of congregations place clergy on a pedestal. Most parishioners look up to them, because the clergy knows so much about god. A member of the clergy is regarded as an intermediary between regular people and the awesome god. The clergy's role is that of a holy person, a worker for the deity. That does place clergy in a special niche.

However, the idea of no god leaves the clergy with no place to go. A member of the clergy becomes a connection to nothing. The clergy member goes from a position of prestige and influence to one of everyday ordinariness.

The member of the clergy is now being faced with the most unwelcome task of admitting that much of his or her preaching may have been mistaken. The entire dedicated life of a clergy member would then appear to have been geared to meaningless ideas. The clergy member is asked to admit that he or she is wrong.

Sure, there is a lot more to being a pastor than emphasizing god. Pastors do some really good things for people. They visit the sick, help those in trouble, etc. But the big part of a clergy's business is still god. Without god, a member of the clergy could probably not function.

I do not expect many clergy members to be convinced after reading this book. They have too much to lose. They have focused on god, lived the idea of god, preached about god, thought they were helping god, etc. They will probably be unable to consider the main points I make. They will consider me an enemy, with wild ideas, not unlike many who have preceded me. They will probably try to suppress the ideas I present in this book. This book will be heresy. I expect the clergy to vigorously defend their positions of prestige and influence. The clergy will no doubt attack the book and the author.

But somewhere in all the resulting verbiage, somewhere in the calm of reason, some clergy members will recognize the inherent truth of what is stated in this book. Deep down inside, they must know that the entire charade is wrong.

Every truly honest member of the clergy should realize that all the ideas in this book can be refuted with one solid fact. Just one firm fact, showing that there is a god, is all that is needed. The reaction to one solid fact would be decisive. It would be similar to my views about extinct dinosaurs. If I were shown one live dinosaur specimen, I would promptly discard my views about dinosaur extinction.

The same response would occur if the reality of god could be decisively demonstrated. One definitive scientific fact is enough. Only one is needed.

But until one solid fact is presented - a compelling, decisive fact - then rational thinking supports my contention that god never existed. God exists only in the imagination of human beings. God is not part of the real world and never will be.

I am aware that the clergy of today are the victims of irrational ideas foisted on them by past generations. They have been deluded much the same way I was deluded. Now it is time to brush off the stifling cobwebs of the past and start thinking clearly. The world will be improved if all of humankind would stick to reality and truth. Let us not continue the great delusion any longer. Religions, as they now operate, should be drastically changed.

I challenge the clergy around the world to come up with one solid fact about the existence of god. But do not besiege me with labels of atheist, blasphemy, etc. Just the facts, and only the facts, will prove convincing. If the clergy cannot come up with one solid fact, then they should be willing to admit that the entire religious structure is on a terribly shaky foundation.

KILLJOY

One of the problems of writing this book is that many people will think of me as a killjoy. I am taking away all the nice, cozy ideas that they love. I am telling them that everything they always wanted and hoped for are a farce.

In a simple way that is correct. But it is not the entire story. Remember that you are the victim of a confidence game. Some people have deluded you. Some people have told you wondrous stories about how marvelous things will be. How you will be protected and loved, how you will live in eternal bliss, etc. But they cannot deliver on these promises. In a sense, each believer is a victim of a confidence game. You believed the stories you were told because you wanted to believe them. You should have recognized that all those marvelous stories and promises were too good to be true. So, do not blame me for depriving you of something you never had.

Who can you blame? You can blame our entire society, and religious leaders in particular. Religious leaders should know better. I am not the killjoy, but only the messenger that brings the bad news.

I am one person who recognized the religious problem and then did something about it. Whatever loss you may feel is one that I have already felt. I was taught many of these religious ideas when I was very young and I did believe them. But in the course of living, I discovered that many of these ideas were empty promises.

When a messenger brings you unpleasant information, do not blame the messenger. During primitive times, some emperors responded to news of an unpleasant disaster by killing the messenger. The messenger was not the cause of the disaster. All the messenger did was report the facts.

So, in a sense, I am the messenger bringing you bad news. But please remember, I am not responsible, many others are.

CONCLUSION

There is a definite conclusion about the god hypothesis that can be made from the contents of this book. As near as I can ascertain, there is not a single scientific fact that supports the god hypothesis. On the other hand, there is a large amount of information that indicates that god does not exist. He doesn't do anything! The conclusion is obvious - god does not exist!

This conclusion is not at the 100% confidence level. Such a conclusion is extremely difficult to make about almost anything. But the conclusion has an extremely high probability of being correct - about 99% or better. There is no firm information that the concept of god, as defined in this book, is real. God appears to be a mental construct of the human mind. God is not a real entity.

As near as can be determined, there are numerous instances where god lets ludicrous things happen. He has let his churches burn down or get destroyed in storms and other natural disasters. He has let his ardent supporters die at the hands of tyrants. He has let huge populations die from hunger and disease. He has allowed warfare to rage for years and years. He has allowed many millions of human beings to die in earthquakes, volcanic eruptions, and severe storms. Even though it is obvious that god should have reacted, he did nothing. He was unwilling or unable to do anything about these situations. If god does exist, he is doing an extremely good imitation of a nonentity. The world functions just as though he is not here. There is nothing to indicate he exists.

Many people will vociferously deny that such a conclusion is valid. But if they cannot produce a compelling fact to decisively show otherwise, their lack of understanding must be considered to be noise, nothing more. Let the din not begin!

Furnish one compelling fact. Nothing else will suffice.

ABOUT THE AUTHOR

Dr. Firsching was born in Utica, N.Y. in 1923. He served for 3 years in the US Army during WWII. He received an A.B. degree from Utica College and master's and doctoral degrees from Syracuse University. He worked for three companies as a research chemist before teaching at the University of Georgia for five years, and Southern Illinois University at Edwardsville for 28 years.

He has 30 scientific publications. Included in these papers were original separations methods for barium and strontium, and the rare earth elements, as well as extensive solubility data for the entire rare earth series. He has maintained a weekly radio show and newspaper column for over 16 years. Mostly scientific subjects were discussed.

He married Shirley Rae Gardner in 1955 and is the father of 6 children and the grandfather of 7. He has active hobbies in rock collecting, bird watching, and nature study. He has traveled extensively in the United States and took sabbatical leaves in California, Arizona, Colorado, and New York. He has visited Europe and South Africa.

Some of the material for the book is taken from a course that he developed called, "The Origins of Life", as well as assorted newspaper columns he had written.